RIDDLE AND BASH

AFRICAN PERFORMANCE AND LITERATURE REVIEWS

BY

CHIN CE

HANDEBOOK
Library of African Writing

RIDDLE AND BASH

AFRICAN PERFORMANCE AND LITERATURE REVIEWS

By

CHIN CE

A Handel Book

RIDDLE AND BASH - African Performance and Literature Reviews

Chin Ce

International Edition
includes notes and works cited bibliography
includes index

For information address:
African Books Network
Handel Books Limited
6/9 Handel Avenue
AI EBS Nigeria WA
Email: handelbook@yahoo.co.uk

Printed in the US and UK
Marketing and Distribution in the US, UK, Europe, N. America (Canada), and Commonwealth countries outside Africa by
African Books Collective Ltd.
PO Box 721
Oxford OX1 9EN
United Kingdom
Email: orders@africanbookscollective.com

Front and Back Cover:
© African Books Network
ISBN: 978-9-7835-0340-3

A Handel Book Publication
Handel Books Ltd.
<http://www.hbooknetworks.com>

Contents

Prefatorial Note

The proceeding is the second volume of essays and book reviews published in journals of African literature since the new millennium. In *Bards and Tyrants*, the first collection which started with a hard look at the nation, I had expressed a wish for a more intense study and appreciation of oral traditions if only to equip scholars of African writings with greater understanding of the challenges of Africa in contemporary modernity. Having only touched upon this aspect of literary criticism in the works of Chinweizu in the first essay collection, I have gone further in this volume, *Riddle and Bash*, to make a case for African orature as the starting point of critical discourse in African literature.

This might be the first detailed observation and study of the African riddle and creative bash activities as oratorical forms that cover the valuable entertainment and corrective educational needs of community. As we join the twenty-first century with the world becoming a global village, writers from Africa will need to preserve the heritage of their people and ensure that the healthy traditions and cultures of Africa are not lost in the march of civilisation. Needless to mention that it suits the interests of some meddlesome interlopers in world affairs that other independent, more original cultures be ignored or entirely subsumed within their own religious and ontological constructs of existence.

I have often argued that the oversight on the part of African intellectuals to take up the challenge of inscribing the values of the continent only to be experts of other literary and cultural products is an abdication of a generational responsibility. And whatever frills that this prodigality garners will always see our children accepting those far-fetched images and outright fabricated notions about Africa yet surviving today in Western writings, films, and documentaries. A good instance is in regard to ancient black heritage. Modern American imagination would still encase the civilisation of the Pharaohs in Middle Eastern traditions presenting the black population not as the dominant line of priest-kings and queens but as slaves and ciphers within an amorphous coexistence of world races; in other words, a distant echo of their unflattering pacification of the American Red Indian.

This however does not deter my hard and honest evaluation of modern Igbo mind, music, culture and religion in the first part of this collection. If my critical judgment in this review leaves much to be desired of Igbo people, it is part of that perspective which seeks to interrogate our legacies and provide adequate proofs that we can still absorb the enduring and beneficent ties of African communion. The subsequent entries on the new literatures and emerging tendencies in literary criticism should also serve as a reminder that the continent is one in spite of different experiences in colonialism, nationalism and post-independent identities. These divisions have benefited only the ever present coloniser and his many new faces who sell us the notion that we can fit well in British, Dutch, Afrikaans, French, et cetera, traditions as far as we de-emphasise our Africanness for the sake of the new modernity. It is gladdening that nothing could be further from the truth. These studies in the literatures of African and black cultures the world over belie such tendencies that deny our true history and contributions among the comity of nations.

January 2010

Acknowledgements

The essays in this volume are collations from literary journals and publisher forums within and outside Nigeria now edited for the African Library Series of Handel Books. I am grateful to the editors of the International Research Confederacy on African Literature and Culture (IRCALC) for the publication 'Riddles and Bash' in *Africa Literary Journal* B4 edition of 2003, and to journal editors of *New Nigerian Poetry* NNP for the 2005 chat series 'Critics of the New Poetry.'

The two series on 'Igbo Mind' had appeared in the theme studies of the *Journal of New Poetry*, NP No. 5 2009 under the title 'Religion, Mind and Music: Egwu Ekpiri in the Millennium.'

More thanks to IRCALC editors for the release of rights to my reviews of recent books of poetry, prose and criticism on African literature featured under the Literature section of this volume. Again this library edition reads better and I am very glad for the opportunity to have all of them in this useful collection.

Dedication

In loving greetings
to my mother Selina,
and my father Bartholomew

A. Performance

1

'Riddle me',

The creative wit of Alaa's children (I)

LITTLE has been written about the riddles of Africa apart from scattered references in some research efforts by Western scholars. But the riddles of African oral traditions might yet survive as a genre of its own, with short diction and imposed meanings, stock devices and stock answers repeated almost word for word in communities where they thrive. Among the children of Alaa[1] the value of the riddle is not just in the thrill or entertainment. There lies abundant wit in the deployment of imagery, epithets and symbolism from the repertoire of Alaa oral tradition. Some of Alaa's progeny today who were regular at the craft had cultivated such dexterity in this artistic form to be recognised as local bards in their own rights.

The creative artist of African tradition is heavily indebted to his immediate environment or larger society. It is the society that provides him with linguistic and literary traditions in terms of a common language or dialect, proverbs and allusions. But this in no way dims his creative genius, drive and originality of his work. By genius we mean the artiste's ability to effect some variations on this body of existing traditional sources at his disposal. 'Some traditions allow for considerable individualistic expression', as Abdulkadir says, '(but) the poet must rely to some extent on traditional forms and structures...and traditional materials in... (his) composition' (18).

In performance the individual talents join the traditional repertoires to make for a unique and pleasing entertainment. Thus riddles are rich with a concatenation of expressions of intrinsic poetic value, and one can agree no less with poets who say that the person who can complete the metaphor and symbols laden in this art genre is well equipped to understand great poetry.

Since riddles, as common property, were never established by any particular individual, they should grow with communal linguistic heritage, taking take their place among the idioms, proverbs and poetry entertainment needs of the community. The great Don John of Alaa confirms that riddle contests during his own time,

> normally come after the farming season when the children had little to do; this contest was there to keep them busy, or when they grow rather restless they are called together and riddles are thrown to them. ('Riddle')

Thus riddles were consequently borne out of communal and educational needs of the community – the need to educate the children and improve their sense of observation of lives around them. De Joe of Okpula[2] explains this enactment in some detail:

> One age-grade sits in a corner, split into two groups. Each group sits in one line, side by side, and facing the other group. Now one member fires the first shot at his counterpart. If the answer proffered is correct, it's one point for the side, otherwise it is one point against the side. Sometimes at the end of it all, are records are tallied to determine the winner. ('Performance')

In African communities social events take their place as both sources of criticism and artistic innovations during performance. For example, a drunkard, a habitually late cook, a scandal or a legal tussle would easily form a most entertaining allusion-laden riddle and bash themes.

Riddle Patterns of Association

A discernible literary trait in the art of riddle performance is the pattern of association of images, objects and life. Parry's formulaic theory sees the formula as a group of words regularly employed under the same metric conditions to express a given essential idea (qtd. in Abdulkadir 18). This definition is implicit to the 'metric condition' of traditional songs or musical renditions. However, the formulaic theory of Parry is not only employed in terms of the 'metric conditions', but the epithet-formula, the noun-formula and verb-formula could also be employed, not in relation to the metrical condition but for what Chukwuma Azuonye calls its 'semantic factor' (2). According to Azuonye, 'traditional epithet is not used for any metrical convenience... the use of formulas, especially epithet formula...is governed by the semantic factor of association rather than any of the mechanical metre' (3).

The latter's position is more plausible with core traditional epithets, symbolism and imagery from which the youthful bards draw their sources adding their own individual talents and enhancing the process of creativity in a pattern distinctive of riddle and bash art. These patterns complement the formulae - usually transferred epithets combined with traditional symbolism in the course of performance. For example, 'ose' (pepper), 'oyogho' (plantain) and 'akummo' (coconut) are symbols of multiple blessings. The little pods of pepper on the plant, the heavy coconut pods, and the cluster of plantains are all symbols of procreation and multiplicity. Thus their manner of presentation in the riddle is laden with transferred epithets, for example:

Riddle me, who is
the rich housewife
with many, many children?

Riddle me, the torch
that makes the whole
world warm.

The seasonal guest
of the whole world.

The coconut tree and the plantain acquire a peculiar character of aloof sequestration from all activity:

Riddle me, who is
the queer woman
who keeps her children
in the heavens.

Riddle me, who is
the foolish maid
that breast-feeds children
over the rafters.

The association of 'breast-feeding' with the coconut differentiates if from the plantain, although both plantain and coconut share similar conditions of high sequestration. A ripe paw-paw is represented thus:

The fair bride who
must not touch –
her husband's mat.

Just as the image of breast-feeding links the coconut with the riddle, so goes the association of the fair bride 'who cannot touch the mat for her husband' traditionally with the ripe papaw that must not be allowed to fall on the dry ground from the tree. We also see the sense of symbolic representations in the moon. The moon in riddles indicates inexhaustible universality and infinity. In riddles there are ways in which the epithet formula of a yam slice, or fire, could be used to describe the moon, for example:

The slice of yam
That feeds the world.

The sun on the other hand is alluded to as the firewood

> that burns unto the
> world without end.

For dramatic effects and improvisations, some sounds in the riddle occupy a distinct traditional acoustic role used in representing particularly related phenomenon. For example, the sound 'kpam' is an acoustic formula that is usually employed for the breaking of wood. Other acoustic device like the sound 'kpum' depict the sound of metal on wood. Generally, the acoustics of riddles are rarely manipulated differently otherwise the meaning is lost. Thus the sound, *kon ti / kon kon kon ti* (meaning 'Crack not kernels / near the pit') may be recited along with the tonal recitation in order that the meaning i.e., the verbal translation mimics fairly the sound, 'kon ti' which in itself is an allophone for the cracking of shells. Similarly, '*tum tum, gem gem*' is an acoustic device for the quick, lithe movement of a rodent. In Alaa Igbo dialect it is a traditional allophone for the smart quick prance of the squirrel. In totality the acoustic formula of 'kpum' for cutting, 'kon ti' for cracking, 'tum tum' for quickness, and 'kpam' for breaking all form part of the source repertoire of the riddles.

Poetics of the Riddle

A further observation of the performance shows the riddle as an elevated poetic play that demands hard mental exercise with its transferred epithets and symbolism. Since these riddles involve the teachings imparted by parents, both players and audience operate from a common source so the repertoire of traditional epithets and allusions are familiar:

gwam nne umu hiri ahugburu gburu	Riddle me, mother with kids all around her side
Gwam nwa bu nna ya uzo taa oji oha	Riddle me, who is the son that took the kola before his father did.
Gwam okoro chara nzu baa n'ohia.	Riddle me, who is the young man in a bush chalked all white.

This group has thrown three darts; it is now the turn of the opposing camp to launch a counter offensive. The questions come in quick succession. If the answer given is incorrect the audience and participants may offer a loud correction:

Gwam agbogho iru mmanu mmanu	Riddle me, the young girl with the fairest face
Gwam nwanyi kpo umu rigoo elu.	the woman whose children are hung in the skies
Gwam otu ibe ji Zuru oha afo.	The slice of yam that feeds every one

There is equally the riddle of sounds and their meanings, similar to what Finnegan calls 'acoustic analogy'(30). This is the ability of the participants to interpret the sounds and rhythms of unnamed objects or events. They are mainly tonal riddles '...in which there is a kind of rhythm in the syllables so that the questions are like two little verses balancing each other in a particular way' (30). They provide poetic lyricism to riddles, for example:

Gwam, kon ti Kon kon ti..	Riddle me *kon ti* *Kon kon ti*

The tonal rendition is done in such a way that it fairly corresponds to the verbal version:

Gwam ereghe re - ti rere.	Riddle me *ereghe re -* *ti rere*

Some of these tonal riddles are also ideophones and sound effects regarding given objects:

Gwam kpom ti Kpo.	Riddle me *kpom ti* *Kpo.*
Gwam kpum! Yoooo!!	Riddle me *kpum!* *Yoooo!!*

Others are traditional onomatopoeia to capture sound and

striking visual effects:

Gwam ihe gbara	What clapped
'kpam!'	'kpam'
Baa n'ohia?	into bush?
Gwam tum tum	Tell me *tum tum*
Gem gem?	*Gem gem.*

Other instances of modification of composition abound. Here the universe of moon, stars and firelight has been manipulated in similar imagistic devices:

Gwam	Tell me
Mpalaka	the lamp which
Zuru uwa nile	travels around the world[5]
Onye ije	The tireless
Nleta uwa.	world traveller

These are the ingenious improvisations that have been employed from the universal attributes of the moon. In the following presentation, the 'smart eye', in the riddle form, is modified from the familiar 'son that took the kola offering before his father' to this other brazen fellow –

who slept with
his brother's first wife

or the

wily man who
seduces the new bride
before her husband.

This variation still retains the formulaic symbolism of 'the clever man' which 'the eye' traditionally occupies in their riddle. Such variations frequently occur and are usually incorporated into the body of traditional texts. Ingenious performers would cultivate some bash (satirical) incidents into riddles:

Okpo nkita	(He taketh his dog
Eje ikpe.	To court
(Chief Mbama)	(Chief Mbama) [answer]

In the above case, Chief Mbama, a man with the notoriety of frequent legal cases, becomes the answer. The point of the satire is the eccentric who sees fit to take his dog to court. There are further examples of local satires through the riddle art form:

Gwam	Riddle me
Okwa nka	the carpenter
Igbeogologo.	of long boxes?

The 'carpenter of long boxes' is a comic euphemism by some Alaa's exuberant youths for the man who makes a living from making coffins. There are allophones which have been created from incidents of such comic nature. The following is a satire of two bed mates:

Gwam	Riddle me
'Piakam	'Piakam
Piaaa!'	Piaaa!'

There are instances where riddles had emanated from some

proverbs commonly used among the elderly members of the lineage. Here the clever children turn these special proverbs and idioms into an evocation. This riddle, for example:

Gwam	Riddle me
Ahu anyuru n'elu	the fart above
Mere anu gwungem?	that stunned the bees?

has obviously come from the traditional proverb that states that a proverb said to a woman is like a fart from a tree top (which none can guess the direction it came). A deeper study of proverbs would reveal device types which are drawn from imagistic, as against prosaic parallels. These often combine to form derivations for the riddle genre particularly when they come as extractions from familiar proverbs of the community:

Prosaic:

'A proverb said to a woman is like a fart from the tree top which none can guess from which direction it came.'

Imagistic:

ahu anyuru n'elu ngwo	the wine tapper's fart
mere anu gwungem	that struck the bees dumb

The above exemplifies a clever attempt to create a riddle and some allophones from the proverb. As the riddle comes from the traditional wine tapping proverb, the bees are made to represent women who from a ridiculing patriarchal sense are not capable of comprehending the 'profundity' of proverbs (even when some women perform better at the art of proverbs than their male counterparts). In this way the long proverb is adapted from its prosaic to a more 'imagistic' parallel. A further example could be drawn from the following proverb and riddle:

Proverb:

Anwu ehihie adighi egbu agwo
(The heat of the twilight is not enough to hurt the snake.)

Riddle:

Oku na-enwu adighi achu agwo?	Fire that never could scare the snake?

Both samples trace the influence of proverbs in some riddles of the people. Ruth Finnegan was therefore correct in her observation that 'among some peoples, riddles may be particularly closely connected with proverbs so that either the answer or even both parts of the riddle are sayings accepted in other contexts as proverbs' (197). However, the distinction between proverbs and riddles lies in the poetry of the latter, the personification of the inanimate, the accordance of anthropomorphism and deployment of deeper levels of meaning and allusions to otherwise simple ideas drawn from the general flora and fauna of the community.

In all, the creative wit of oral riddles and bash forms, like oral literature in Africa, is a continually expanding and enhancing totality, with lots of opportunity for variations eloquence, dramatic devices and individual artistry which go with the performance of this most intriguing art. No wonder that it was deservedly prized among the people of Alaa in the times it flourished.

2

'Bash them',

The creative wit of Alaa's children (II)

Agreeably 'performance is a doing art' (Hagler 98), and 'an overt behaviour as a realisation of an underlying knowledge on the part of the speaker' (Hymes 18). For those children of Alaa who grew up witnessing and participating in the robust and rowdy bash sessions of their age grades, knowledge implies the traditional ability to interpret and recreate incidents realised by elaborate dramatic enactments.

In those days a bash session was usually performed among age-grades during the moonlit frolics. It was organised in a way usually involving boys on one side and girls on the other. As De Joe says,

> Girls stand in a row, facing the boys who swagger defiantly before them. This usually marks the end of the session. It

> begins when one of the boys makes some rude advances to a female counterpart, and she retorts with an abuse. The others remonstrate sharply and the battle of wits begins. It usually ends with all returning to their homes, claiming victory over their opponents. ('Performance')

Nowadays moonlight plays and dances have virtually disappeared from African towns and villages. This has limited the practice and enjoyment of an art that was once a way of life for the people. But these days too public performances are more spontaneous. Two youths may engage in a performance contest taking notes to determine the winner where there is no audience.[4] However, the presence of an audience enlivens the performance more.

Here is a typical occasion of bash performance: A cluster of small groups in a public tap; there are few adults, a number of young people with an admixture of male and female sexes; there are less conscious divisions of participants in opposing camps, in other words, a free-for-all session. So members of the audience are participants at the same time. Typically, a player finds his supporters among those who mock his opponent. Quite dramatically, one supporter might turn around to be an antagonist, pitching his tent with the group gaining the louder ovation. This *volte face* adds boisterous laughter to the game:

Challenger 1: To Opponent.	(Translation)
Chidi maka mkpuru rice	Chidi For one grain of rice,

ka iji gbaa nna gi ekpuruke n'ahia ukwu taa	You threw your father In a wrestle today.

(Chidi's reply)

Ohoo? Maka ibe akidi Otu-ibe akidi Igbara nne gi n'ala	Really? And you for a been-seed wrestled your mother to the ground.

Now another participant, Uka, wades in, pitching his tent with Chidi.

Uka to Challenger 1:	Translation:
Eze mhuru gi n'onu Dika foku ekwensu ji-ata ugba.	The teeth in your mouth are like the roasting prongs of the devil.

Challenger 1:	Response:
Iya! Obu ya kpatara Iji eme onu Ka ina-ami Ndi opo avu. Na nti gi-a Buchaa otua Dika afo ime onwa asaa.	Oh yeah? and that is why your mouth looks like you kissed a leper's sores. And your chin is bulging like a seven-month pregnancy.

The audience-narrator interaction provides a common spur

for the creative ingenuity of the youths. It is now a free-for-all and highly entertaining spree of verbal bashing and mockery:

Ugbua kedu onye Onu ya na-esi Dika ogwe juru eju?	Now who is it That his mouth reeks Like the pit latrine?
Ma ahu mhuru Gbara okporo iji Anya gharii.	You farted on the street And even the flies Went rigid with fright.
Lee ka ukwu Na-ahu gi ririri Dika oche ndi Anu odogwo.	But why does your leg Shake so badly Like the rickety table Of stale-meat butchers.
Dada, isi gi yiri nke udele Mmiri mara.	Dada, your hair Reminds me of a vulture Soaked in the rain.
Obu ya mere Iji dowe onu Ka nwa mkpi	And that is why Your nose is hung like a billy goat's...

Any of the above usually wins from both audience and participants a loud, complimentary remark: 'heee!' or 'kooo!' for disapproval - which confirms the statement that for the performers 'their greatest appeal lies in their lively spontaneity and the performer's unquestioned familiarity with the traditional element of his art' (de Graft 10):

The test of creative wit is that one does not lack the verbal dart to throw at his opponent in this admix of imaginative improvisations. Even when core traditional imagery are exhausted, participants begin to improvise with contemporary incidents in the community. Individual artistry differs among the youths, and it is this peculiar attribute in each of the participants that informs the different 'techniques of ornamentation' (Abdulkadir 30).

Mgbeke, nwa Mgborie	Mgbeke daugher of Mgborie
Ezilam ukwu gi- a	No need to swing
Ukwu ndanda gi	your hips to me
Agaghi ekoli nke	That ant-waist of yours
Dee Mathias	Could hardly rouse old Mathias

Techniques of ornamentation are more prolific in the bash 'battle' as a spontaneous activity that demands quick thinking. But behind all the continuum of spontaneity and innovation, traditional texts abound from the overflow of exuberant creative genius. In fact these young adults start from the familiar traditional sources then make their own improvisations with exercise of their wide imaginative powers aimed, of course, at outwitting one another. It has been explained that 'traditional African life in general is rich in poetic expressions... in a sense that is far reaching, for they are not only spontaneous and realistic but also beautiful' (Egudu 57). It is also the spontaneity of its action that marks the beauty and liveliness of most African performances.

Imagery of Bash Contests

During the bash session of this cultural fair, a range of traditional core images are deployed in performance. Alaa youths are mostly informed by their early or original knowledge of the traditional similes and metaphors acquired from many series of performances. The allusions are generally ludicrous, highly exaggerated but suggestive of underlying meanings, for example:

> Hail everyone !
> Did you know
> For one grain of rice
> Nathan has wrested the throne
> from his own father?

This bash has a dramatic effect by its suggestion of greed and avarice, which is being countered by an even more aggravating or ludicrous 'offence':

> Yes but we also know
> That for one been seed
> Ekwedike wrestled his mother
> At the market square.

Ekwedike's act in this counter-fire profanes womanhood, a more serious traditional offence than the former. In both 'rice grain' and 'bean' seed are symbols of grandly taste. From a wider perspective, this might mean the superimposition of the acquired taste over the more traditional values of reverence for father and mother. The implication of greed is seen in the very mean proportion of the diet – 'a grain of rice' and a 'bean seed'. There is the further depiction of Ike's mouth that '.. .reeks/ like the pit latrine /very near full...' or smells like the 'fart on a tree top/ that shocked the fly dumb.' These are strong metaphors of unpleasant health conditions or poor personal hygiene. The motif of ugliness or complete lack of beauty is usually present in most traditional references to the white man's appearance and manners. In fact, the stock opening device in a bash session: "hail him sir!" is a fallout of the district officer's image under the colonial administration. This probably lies behind all these images that always recur in the bash:

> The old vulture
> drenched in the rain
>
> Your chin
> like the bulge
> of pregnant Maria.
>
> your teeth
> the roasting fork
> of the devil himself.

These colonial portraits of physical incongruity along with their varied manners of presentation, make up the children's satirical bouts against their opponents. Elements of Christian myths ('fork of the devil') are sprinkled freely to spice the traditional ridicule and contempt for the new religion that had subverted the old ways. These allusions have come to stay in the course of more socialising experiences, thus their knowledge also drawn from the core traditional repertoire that are used to tease, taunt and so correct young behaviours and mannerisms.

Call-Response Dramatic Patterns

The pattern of riddle call-and-response is a traditional stock-opening device of drama always observed in the bash performance. The challenger rises to the initiative by calling the name of his opponent. The opponent who then accepts the challenge replies 'Ehee!' along with the audience, who all anticipate the first 'attack'. It is an original device which is used to prepare the participants for the questions and abuses involved in the contest. Every participant begins in this way until the excitement gathers momentum and the stock call-response is abandoned briefly. This especially occurs in the bash contests which, like the riddle, over time, are greatly enriched by such performers' excited contests. In this stock formula of opening call and response, ingenious children bring their talents to play. For instance, prolonging the call is an art that achieves some dramatic Here, for example, Chidi not just takes on his opponent, but also invites the audience:

Call:	Tuorum ya nu Saa!	Call:	All hail him 'Sir!'
Resp:	Saa!	Resp:	Sir!

Call:	Tuorum ya nu Saa!	Call:	All hail him 'Sir'.'
Resp:	Saa!	Resp:	Sir!
Call:	Tuorum ya nu Saa!	Call:	All hail him 'Sir!'
Resp:	Saa! Saa! Saa!	Resp:	Sir! Sir! Sir!

This deliberate rolling and prolongation of the call might be accompanied by a dramatic battle-cry. The intention will be to create some comic effect that eventually wears down the other side and throws them off their guard when the shot is suddenly released. In some instances the stock call may be intoned along a familiar lyric. This enhances the dramatic and entertainment value of the contest.

Other dramatic gesticulations feature prominently, apart from the mock dance and battle-cry. As in the riddle where a conscious attempt by a participant may be made to dramatise, for instance, what clapped 'kpam' into the bush, so in the bash will many a performer attempt an act out a part of social, political and even religious incident. In a riddle performance, a cue for the exclamation 'kpam' may go with a hand clap. In the bash session, the 'ant-waist' or the nose that looks like that of the billy goat, the flatulent chin, could all be acted out in a way that enhances or aggravates the ugliness of the physical body. Of course these effects are easily achieved by ingenious ones who have the peculiar ability to twist some parts of their bodies to achieve the desired effect.

By the sheer power of imagination, and in their vociferous excitement, the youths of Alaa through their riddle and bash performances display artistry and ingenuity; and by exploring original traditional patterns or formula, they also recreate history and incidents, reworking, refurbishing and enhancing their oral heritage.

Africa Literary Journal, 2003.

3

Igbo Mind,

Music, Culture and Religion (I)

Throughout the Dark Ages of mediaeval Europe, Christendom with its Inquisitions and holy wars had sought to exterminate or drive underground other ancient belief systems and cultural practices that opposed its pantheons and theories of creation and world government. Despite the increase in secularisation of society in the seventeenth and eighteenth centuries with the discovery of gravitation and revolution of the earth, et cetera, Christian religious bigotry held sway and continued its attacks on such progressive movements in human understanding which dared to bring the searchlight on its contradictory doctrines on the structure of the universe. From a veneer of Christian religious benevolence in the eighteenth century this practice continued through nineteenth century European violent conquest and colonisation of many parts of the world, including Africa, and the disruption of economic, material, spiritual and ethical structures upon which traditional cosmogony endured. African nation states have since emerged from the European contact to become artifices and colonies of Europe existing for economic administrative purposes of Imperialism with no respect for cultural or filial bonds of their own people.

Nigeria became one of these countries in West Africa that came into existence for the convenience of economic exploitation by the colonial British in 1914. The colonial government under Lord Lugard amalgamated the regions of North and South knowing the problems of Nigeria's pluralistic composition. Early before independence was handed down to natives in 1960 colonial writers had admitted of "difficulties in the way of preserving unity in multinational, multi-religious Nigeria".[1] This problem, compounded by British divide-and-rule policy and a visionless administrative bureaucracy under the charge of their governor-generals from Lugard through Robertson, culminated in perennial turmoil for the hundreds of ethnic nationalities that made up the new nation state.

Even as a republic from 1963, Nigeria continued to wobble in confusion. An undemocratic oligarchy had emerged and there began a reign of historical distortions in the political and cultural scheme of domination bequeathed by the colonial European government. These tendencies are now entrenched within succeeding generations of Nigerian leadership and their tribal cleavages by way of wily competition for advantages in Nigerian natural and political environment.

With the exportation of oil in the early seventies, after the 1967-1970 war, Nigeria under a cavalier and irresponsible military regime, increased its reputation for corruption in the Third World. Sudden wealth from exportation of crude oil to Europe and America brought a new oligarchical mentality of abject neglect of natural endowments. In both the leaders and the led was seen the contempt for agriculture and honest labour. A grand fossilisation of culture and tradition became the pastime of government braggadocios in a fuddled vision to catch up with the modern world in technology and infrastructural advancements. With Nigeria's immediate failure from inception, Africa's destiny was subsequently altered for the worst case scenarios that followed.

Christianity and Igbo Mind

The Igbo and neighbouring cultures of the south east of Nigeria had their fair share of the colonial debacle. In the race for acquisition of Western education which seriously altered black destiny in the twentieth century they were not left out. They have also been most vicious in embracing Western Social Darwinism along with the predatory survivalism of Capitalism and its attendant deformation of native culture and tradition.

While the Hausa and Yoruba reconstructed their Bayajidda and Oduduwa legends of ancestry, for reasons not entirely alien from contempt for oral traditions, early Igbo scholars seemed to spurn their own origin tales. They were rather eager to dismiss what they called "tribal myths of so-called common historical origins" of the people.[2] Others had surmised insights as to Igbo origins in the assurance that "a certain measure of civilisation" had flourished in some parts of Igboland as early as the 9th century AD.[3] However, a very important historian, Kenneth Onwuka Dike, was the first to record that the region of Igbo speaking towns on the banks of the lower Niger holds oral traditional claims of origins from the four tribes of Atani, Ogwu, Obuche and Umunankwo.[4] There also abound evidence of kinship among Igbo, Yoruba, Hausa and adjacent tribes of the delta in the widespread influence of Nok culture which, scholars agree, are also part of many of the "cultural characteristics of later West African art".[5] Beyond these is a gulf of amnesia from which the Christian colonists claimed to have sprung the tribes to a certain awareness of their existence.

All of humanity generally have often been bound to amnesia. Accounts of reversed polarities of the earth indicate that most of the Neolithic ages suffered some blank moments in history when serial cataclysms engulfed the planet and wiped out more than three quarters of earth's inhabitants.[6] Still the black world has been left with cultural, physiological and ontological evidence with which history may be reconstructed. Most glaring is the physical and cultural characteristic of the race. This cultural unity of Africa has been constructed from evidence of its ancient priestly crafts, its ancient science of corporeal, interplanetary motions, advanced religious rituals of spiritual cleansing, immediacy of divine communion and reverence for the Supreme represented by Sun and Lightning deities.[7] Within these characteristics the Igbo along with thousands of Africa's ethnic nationalities have found their rightful place of origin.

Nonetheless, with Christianity- and Islam-dominant prejudice, followers of these religions have begun to reject the historical connections to Africa's ancient religious and metaphysical systems. For them, works by true scholars such as Anta Diop, Soyinka, Chinweizu, Awoonor, Sofola, Asouzu, Enekwe and Emezue[8] in the alignment of Africa with its unity of cultural and spiritual heritage could well remain in the closet of modern religious bigotry.

It is the fashion nowadays for Igbo writers, singers, poets, musicians, and political leaders to queue behind Semitic racialism anchored upon the sole-messianic doctrine in their search for history and memory. The procedure is to sieve popular passages and comments left by slave ship captains, merchants, rebel leaders, and obscure passages in bible testaments to trace their lineage with the Semitic tribes of the eastern Mediterranean.

As noted in the beginning, the sole-messianic doctrine had come to Africa with European colonisation of the land. Like its Capitalist economic practices, this doctrine corrupted Africa, desecrated its traditions, atrophied a natural and steady progress in civilisation and vandalised its ancient monuments of art and spirituality. Currently in the consciousness of an Igbo artiste, whether of poetry, music or fiction, is a split schizophrenic mind where the one is ruefully aware of its African identity and the other seeks a new made ancestry in the hope to gain admittance into a paradisiacal afterlife of Semitic and Aryan configurations. As they pay homage to their imported religions, the events in the barren land of Judea barely two thousand years ago acquire a strange bearing upon their own history.

Going by its blatant revisions of history in favour of its own religious beliefs and assumptions, it is doubtful that the Christian world will ever own up that the Semitic records from which the doctrine of faith subsists were the constructs of mythmaking *pseudepigrapha*. The great Fela Anikulapo Kuti even stated, and it had sounded like profanity, that "Christianity and Islam...are only artificial religions, and the reason why Islam and Christianity are spreading all over Africa, we know, is to exploit the people".[9]

Since Nigeria and her neighbours now bear the stock of Christianised, Arabised and even Frenchified black races content with depreciation of ancient cultural and spiritual heritage in favour of historically violent traditions, we may not have seen the last of Igbo scholars sieving through Middle Eastern records in search of ties with the Jews of Palestine. This tendency to spurn evidence that have their ancestry firmly rooted in African traditions[10] is an African prodigality that thrives further in dogged attempts at incorporating the ugly blemishes of Western civilisation within their own modernity. Current Nigerian movie tabloids are steeped in retarded and base mimicry of America's Hollywood. In them the bunch of "actors" and "producers" delight in the pillory of traditional religion as backward, tyrannical and evil, while Christian materialism takes on the act of *Dues ex Machina* around the miserable conflicts they project on video "to the Glory of God."

Normally these tendencies are wrought from the Red-Cross complex that Christianity liberated the region. Some writers have told of educational, medical and useful social and humanitarian services rendered by Western Christian missions in Igboland early in the twentieth century[11] and the gallant humanitarian efforts of the group with the criminal blockade of Biafra during the civil war. But the argument by traditionalists that Christianity enslaved, rather than liberated, the Igbo mind holds true in more recent developments. For whereas tradition had emphasised individual and collective responsibility in social progress or malaise, the Christian ethic is an offer of escape through a sole-messiah whose configurations were craftily taken from ancient Pagan motifs. As a consequence of this religious fraud the consolidation of the doctrines of Christianity and Westernisation in Africa and elsewhere has seen sophistication in criminality, the brazen pursuit of Western materialism in the guise of salvation, a mistaken notion that divinity is conferred to only one man, and that redemption is given free in spite of culpable historical actions and moral wickedness of their crusaders.[12]

Very few biblical scholars and interrogators have been bold enough to show the misinformation, snide and forgery in Old and New testament doctrines and records of history. Fewer still show them as tendentious documents to uphold Zionism, racism and domination through fear and spiritual inferiority among all who profess and uphold their tenets in the Third World.[13]

Somehow a minority scientific community of Europe whose counterparts in religion and politics brought the Bible to Africa hold their religion in subtle contempt. Church pews remain empty and wholesale deference for doctrinal injunctions whether from the Qumran apocalypses or the Papal Bull of Roman Catholicism are, at best, superficial.

Yet the doctrines are absolute truth in Third World Igboland.

The Igbo are endowed with a language unique to the tropical rainforests of the Congo basin which is not even Amharic, the official language of Ethiopia belonging to the Semitic branch of Afro-Asiatic languages. But their Christians are required to pride in a Jewish heritage and join in the abasement of the Pharaohs of Egypt who, as the epic tale goes, "persecuted" a wandering tribe "chosen by God" to "civilise" the world. A few great thinkers have dared to point out the lie of the Bible record of contact with the ancient world holding Zionism blameworthy in extreme historical fabrication and reductionism.[14] Some have queried why there was no mention in this holy record of the great pyramids of Egypt at Gaza and their institutional roles in the spiritual training of initiates from all over the known world. And why, rather, Egypt's stock of ancient codices, libraries and artefacts which the armies of Alexander, Caesar and Napoleon plundered severally, have all been embalmed in mystified prejudice. Was this so that the world may forget forever that civilisation's religious, musical and artistic traditions which adored the creator of the universe and composed hymns in adoration and emulation of the qualities of the Supreme Being? Was it to erase the facts of those ancient teachings of resurrection and return of the savants which Judaism and Christianity had imitated and copied in their later writings?

Demonising the mystery teachings bequeathed the world from ancient Egyptian centres of learning still continues in contemporary American science and historical fictions. But it is more daunting that this cultural flagellation is rapidly upheld in musical renditions and cultures of African societies. Today, among Igbo artistes who profess to play the traditional highlife or such older music forms, a good instance might be Chief Maduka, a.k.a. Morrocco, the stylish and popular celebrant of the traditional Igbo *Ekpiri or Ekpili* musical whose *Vision 2000* VCD proclaims him "Eze Egwu Ekpili" (The King of Ekpili music).

Ekpili Music and Igbo Mind

Maduka's *Egwu-Ekplli* comprises stanzas that contain themes of spiritual, philosophical and material significance in Igbo worldview. In the call-and-response pattern of Igbo traditional music, there is always the chorus which serve to reinforce the theme or argument and, somehow, the philosophical mood of the songs. The singer begins in the best tradition of this music form with a consideration of the world and the role of divine forces in human destiny:

Oo ije enu, Oo ije enu	Life's journey
siri ike	Oh the climb is so hard
Onye kere uwa,	Creator of the world,
Oo enu uwa	Oh the world

ekwe mmeta cannot be pleased.

Of significance is the stoicism and pessimism of the song embedded within the context of benighted humanity. Igbo cosmological polarity balance, finally broken by the foreign religions, is now submerged in Christian dualism where the forces are in vicious opposition. In ancient times, the masculine-feminine, or negative-positive lines, may have been guarded by the impartial arbitration of gods and their messengers. A violation of the cosmic order entailed some payment in restoration. In other words good and bad were never absolute but relative. This was borne from the understanding that the entire cosmos is so complex and interwoven that one act somewhere has an implicit and corresponding effect elsewhere, and the original harmony, also called Divine love, may be restored by placatory and beneficent deeds.

On the contrary, Christianity was intent on subverting what it perjured pagan, but more arcane, spiritual directions. So they not only confuted the celestial harmony with their own stories of irreconcilable battles between the forces, and among the elements, in which a sole-redeemer emerges victorious, but sustained this non-cosmic ideal in an intricate play of doctrinal cajolements. Its flaws have nonetheless left its adherents bewildered and confused as to the replication of evil in the world in spite of the good news of glorious salvation through one man. Yet the Igbo artiste sings:

Oyim Chi na-eme eze, nwannem

Okwa isi na Chi na-eme eze
Emeẹ elu mee ala ilo na asili gadilili
Anugo Chukwu tili mmadu nile nélu uwa
N'oya ko osi aga

Ah, God makes a king, my brother
Ah yes, God makes a king
if you're high or low, rancour will exist
It is God who put humans on earth
And that is how it goes...

Traditionally, in the first, place "enu" ("hill") is symbolic of the climb upward in progress and self knowledge. "Ije enu" is then an equivalent of the pilgrim's progress filled with temptations, trials and reversals. But later in the song "Ije enu" becomes "Ije ego" the pursuit of money and other material acquisitions in the world:

Oo ije ego; Oo ije ego
sili ike
Ole eje eme uwa;
Oo elu uwa
ekwe mmete.

The climb to wealth,
Oh, the journey's so hard
What do we do this world?
Oh the world
has no solution.

Furthermore, the idea that "Chi na-eme eze" (God who makes fortune) as projected in Morocco's *Ekpili* marks the era of cosmic absolutism imposed by Christianity which never sat well with traditional thought. Igbo philosophy once held that men make their destiny: "when a man says yes his Chi also affirms" although in few cases a man's *chi* may say nay in spite of his affirmations as Achebe had told in *Things Fall Apart*. But Morocco argues an infused concept of a chosen people, the beloved of God, or Gods' special. This has since gained ground at religious extravaganzas, in the churches, playgrounds and public spheres. A state and other local centres in Nigeria have claimed to be God's very own in spite of the moral depravity of their governors, local chairs and retinue of followers. It is the narcissist Davidic dominion-complex, of a child shepherd who is magically transformed to war hero by God, which abides in the logic that since God's blessing is absolute, then for any claimant, including the retinue of politicians, businessmen and fraudsters, or even the inspired or genetically gifted artist that Chief Maduka thinks of himself, there can be no serious fallouts of individual responsibility in a divine mandate. Thus "their enemies all mock in vain".

Maka na onye chukwu gozili agozi eze ka obu
Ime elu me ala nwannem ina-eme na nkiti
Onye chukwu gozili agozi eze ka obu
Ime elu me ala nwannem ina-eme na nkiti

For the one God has blessed is made king
Whatever you do, my brother, you do in vain
The one God has blessed is made king
Whatever you do, my brother, you do in vain

There is an engram in Igbo religious thought that when a songster and his many choruses proclaim "God's blessing" or His crowning, this is only a euphemism for sudden power and great material possessions. Such wealth, usually from the dubious constructs of Nigerian politics, are unquestioned by scores and hundreds of Christian priests, Muslim Imams and glorious praise singers who support the criminality of their leaders as the gift of God.

A fourth point must be noted that Morocco's regrettable world of little or no positive destiny in all subsequent movements is quite alien in construct and can have pertained to monastic traditions of early Christianity and Qumran communities from which the former's tenor and vision are drawn.[17] This theme further contradicts the bustling notion of exalted (privileged) ones he had canvassed early on. In spite of God's blessings, still the world is bad and there is nothing that can be done to make it better. In other words man in his nature is hopeless; redemption is by divine intervention. But even this serious Puritan proposition also turns hilarious and banal in the mouth of the Igbo singer:

Umu uwa geem nti	People of the world listen
o wele ife m ga-agwa unu	I have something to tell you
Mka ihe anyam na-afu nélu	Because what my eyes see
uwa	in this world
Onum afulu iko ya	My mouth dare not speak it
Imee mma ino nókwu	If you do well you are in trouble
Imee njo níno nókwu	If you do bad you're in trouble

Maduka's *Ekpili* music philosophy, in the best of methods of Christianity and its confused understanding of African spirituality, laments the tragic order on earth and the avarice of its inhabitants allied with the consciousness of conflict, tension and supremacy battles of good and evil. The world is bewildered and his Igbo religious mind proffers no idea as to a remedy or response to a situation that is such a hopeless mystery:

Owele ife iga-eme wee meta uwa mma Imma mma níno nókwu I joo njo níno nókwu-o Iwee ego níno nókwu I daa ogbenye o ka gi njo Kedu zia ihe aga-eme uwa odi mma?	You cannot please the world by any deed If you're good you're in trouble If you're ugly you're in trouble If you're rich you're in trouble If you're poor it's worse for you What then can be done to make the world well?
Onye nwele ego nozi n-afufu Onye enwele ego tolo ato. Na nwanyi mala mma kotelu okwu Onye jolu njo no náfufu anya	A rich man is in danger A poor man is in a rut A pretty woman has bought trouble And the ugly one is in deep envy
Kedu zi ebe anyi ga-agbaba Nwannem okwa uwa siri ike.	Where then shall we run to? My brother the world is tough.

And later when the Igbo singer admits his benign scepticism as to the innocence of any member in a generally retarded cosmogony, it is not because everyone claims his or her innocence by the popular saying, “My hands are clean.” The artiste wonders who is guilty, 'where are those whose hands are not soiled'? simply to project his hypothesis of a sleazy universe:

Ijuo nwoke	Ask the man he says
osi na ya ji ofo	he has good cause
Ijuo nwanyi	Ask the woman she says
osi na ya ji ofo	she has good cause
Maka na onye obula	Everyone says his hands
si n'aka ya di ocha	are clean white
I ga-agwam	Can you tell me whose
onye aka ya di oji?	hands are soiled black?

Yet another rendering contradicts public opinion and flips the perspective on corruption in society. Maduka turns from inculpation of Nigerian leadership to focus on the collective guilt of the led in the perpetration of fraud and bribery by "Nigeria Police".

Ebele na-emerem ndi Polisi	I pity the Policeman
Ihu Polisi	If you see Police
meelu ya ebere	have pity on him
Meelu ya ebere,	Have pity on him,
meelu ya ebere	have pity on him
na mgbara agba onu	For the censure of
ana-agba Polisi akalika.	Police is just too much.

His thesis is that the Police of Nigeria are to be pitied for their moral dilemma on the question to take or not to take bribes. This dilemma is imposed by fellow nationals who remain implacable and would disparage occasional police dedication to duty as well as their wonted dereliction of responsibility. It is a useful perspective to the general moral decay that has everyone guilty:

Onye dala iwu ma na Odara iwu
Polisi jide onye dala iwu obido yoowa polisi abegi
Abegi abegi a no go do again o
Abegi abegi a go give you one thousand
Abegi abegi a go give you three thousand
Abegi abegi a go give you five thousand
Polisi nara ego asi na ha na-eri ngali
Oju inalu ego asi na fa bu Polisi ajoka
Kedu ihe ha ga-eme ka owe di unu mma

The miscreant knows he broke the law
Police arrests the miscreant, he starts to plead
Please, please, I won't do that again
Please, please, I will give you one thousand!
Please, please, I will give you three thousand!
Please, please, I will give you five thousand!
Police takes the money you say they take bribe
He refuses the offer, you say how wicked of him
What can be done for it to be well with everyone?

Meanwhile with the absence of any remedy that can satisfy the populace, we can return to the plague of modern materialism as the subject of musical contemplation. In the subsequent movement, it might seem that the singer only bemoans that the days of good neighbourliness and of our so-called communal brotherhood where neighbours looked out for one another are gone. However, the irony of this lament on our modern condition is on the poor. In order words, modern Igbo culture actually laughs at the poor and wretched who are left behind "Ïje-enu" and "Ïje-ego": the race for wealth and possessions which is always being couched in overtones of religious devotion. Thus the new moral of the Igbo race as exemplified in the public conduct and private lives of their military and civilian representatives, and which has made them losers in every national equation, has been "every man for himself, and God for us all":

> Akwa onye nwee ego o nwee nwanne
> Onye na-enwelu ego o di-enwe onye nso nélu uwa
> Onu ubiam ona-azo onye oga-achi?
> Nwannem uwa ka anyi na-eme
>
> Is it not the wealthy that have kindred?
> The abject poor, do they have kindred?
> Can a hungry mouth look for whom to rule?
> My brother we are just making out in the world.

4

Igbo Mind,

Music, Culture and Religion (II)

Before Chief Maduka Morocco became very well known for his *Ekpili* musical dance performance, E*kpiri* music was already fairly popular in Imo, Anambra and Wawa regions of Igboland. Noted as part of *Ekpe* dance,[15] although *Ekpe* is a religious cult of more general function in Igbo societies, *Ekpiri* was popular with older and young music traditions. In theory, all the elements of functional art and the responsibility of its custodian in nourishing the educational and aesthetic well being of society abound in this musical form.

Morocco brought humour and laughter into his version of the music with his poignant observations on Igbo social life. But as it grew in popular acceptance, Morocco's *Ekpili* turned into a medium of praise singing for the well-to-do of his society with snippets of Christian religious moralising that barely mask the celebration of Igbo acquisitiveness and consumerism. This makes his role and that of like Igbo artistes as traditional custodians of heritage a vague and distant possibility.

Chief Samuel Aniefomendun, also called "Onwa na Ogidi" (The Sun at Ogidi), while speaking of Morocco in accolades of proverbs and religious undertones, hints at the subject of the creative artist in his immediate environment or community:

> Ya nwa amutalu nkea amuta, kama osi na Chi. Owulu onyinye... Ifu osisi gbalu mgborogwu, gbalu mgborogwu. Odi ka ije ku akuku nókwute. Ima na oga-epurepu. Nkea bu onwelike lalukata ula, obia. echi nile egwu adaa. Obulu nke makasilinu.[15]
>
> He did not learn this, rather it comes from God. Being a gift, you see, a great tree is a great tree. It is like planting on a rock. You know it will wither. (But) this one, he might just wake up from sleep, and tomorrow, here comes the music. That is the most beautiful part (of his talent).

The rigmarole nevertheless throws some light on their perception of art as a gift, or an inspiration, not a question of learning and studious application. In other words, society recognises "akalaka" (talent) which inspires and moulds a performer, artist, leader or scholar in an ennobling direction of individual and communal wholeness. This is not unlike the Platonian utilitarianism which encourages honour of parents and reverence for gods, and the forging of moral virtues through the arts. This ancient traditional moral is that ease and perfection come with talent applied studiously for community benefit. But when Chief Maduka is likened to a great tree with sturdy tap roots, and one who could awake from a nap and render us a musical masterpiece, this belief turns more favourably towards the Nigerian system where every service seeks that flash of dreamlike religious inspiration that endows success and wealth irrespective of practice, learning and discipline.

It is not uncommon for Igbo patrons to turn to praise singing like their artistes do. Patronage of the arts goes a long way in tradition. Artistes working on one or other professions in their secular lives, may, at times, need the assistance of patrons whose financial, social and material supports generally enhance the survival of the service. They acknowledge their benefactors at the beginning, or during, their performance with a dedication, greeting or praise. In his performance Morocco like other Igbo artistes such as Warrior, Osadebe and Oliver de Coque, would veer off in long tangent to pay tributes to sponsors of his musical *Ekpili* who had showered him with valuable gifts and approbation.

Below, another of Chief Maduka's patrons, Chief Ngozi Nwaokpagu, "Omeloha na Nise" ("Benefactor of Nise People"), extols his musical prowess. Like Aniefomendun, the chief also draws the religious card for the Igbo singer's artistic brilliance:

> Morocco bu Chukwu-na-enye eze. Chukwu nyere Morrocco egwu, nye ya ife ona-eme. (Ya) bu na egwu bu akaraka; egwu si na Chi. O wee welu na-aga níhu. Oburo onye obula puta otiwe egwu. Morrocco bu ife Chukwu nyelu. and O 'talent' ka

osi aga. uwa nile wee malu ya.

Morocco is King-endowed-by-God. God had given him the gift of music, his craft. That is to say music is talent; music comes from God. He has progressed very well with music. Music should not be an all-comers affair. Morocco is what God has endowed. And it is this talent that marks him forward. And the world knows him for this.

Here again the idea of divine election for the arts is inflated with local and imported religious ideals. Usually, a calling that runs in the genetic history of their custodians progresses with some formal apprenticeship and training. But Chief Maduka, tracing his musical career and experience, admits of very little formal training. As he claims:

Otewo mgbe mji bido egwu, maka na ebidorom egwu na nwa. Ogem na-aga akwukwo nífe dika 1963, mka no núno akwukwo obere , anam eje akwukwo na-eti egwu. Otego aka mu na egwu. Etiberem ya wee tolu...
Maka na nnem gulu, nnam gulu. nna mama mu gulu nke di egwu, fa no Oka. nna mama mu bu nwogbo gulu egwu nke di egwu. kama na ife melunu bun a egwu ha bu Óguta ora eke'aguta enwero ihe eji egwu eme.

It has been long since I started playing music; I started right from childhood. Sometime in 1963 when I attended primary school, I was playing music. It has been long, this talent of mine. I have played music till my adult years...
For my mother sang, my father also sang. My mother's father was a great singer at Awka (Anambra State of Nigeria) My father's mother was a great singer too. But those days their

music was public domain: there was no profit in the trade.

The "King of *Egwu-Ekpili*" does not elaborate on his epiphany in music aside from the above claim that his practice is unique to his lineage and that he has espoused this music even farther than other eminent singers had done with their own music forms; he says:

> Anam agwa ndi ka bidoro Egwu Ekpili ebido ha gbaa mgbo mee egwu ekpiri ka oburu nke ndi Igbo. maka na ndi Awusa na-eti "Gwoge", Yoroba na-eti "Juju" ma na egwu Ekpiri bu nke ndi Igbo. Mwee gbaa mgbo mee ya bu egwu ka ogbagotaa nélu, ka ndi ocha na-agba ya, ka Awusa na-agba ya, ka Yoroba na-agba ya.
>
> I am telling the upcoming generation of *Ekpili* singers to strive and make the music the pride of Igboland. Because the Hausa have their "Gwoge" dance, the Yoruba have their "Juju" dance but *Ekpiri* is an Igbo thing. I have strived to make this music highly prized, so even the white man would dance to it; everyone Hausa, Yoruba and the like.

Egwu Ekpili Costume and Dance Performance

We are gratified that Maduka's *Ekpili* performance in VCD retains a glimpse of this honoured though unrecorded musical entertainment of the Igbo people in spite of its Nigerian version of Hollywood entertainment with imported graphics of modern cityscape, video effects, flashing colours and lighting animations. The *Ekpili* song and dance performance led by Maduka Morocco is elaborate with staid, forward and backward patterns. A group of men in long decorative gowns, red caps, large red beads and broad circular fans held in their hands exhibit their prestige and status in the land. Their regal manners evoke an aura of priesthood. The distinguished singer, Chief "Dr." Maduka, leads the procession. He appears severally in rich, darkly robes and a jumper with golden embroideries. At times this proud holder of several titles can also be seen donning a short hat; beads deck his neck and right arm to confirm his chieftaincy. At other moments in the performance he appears in green and white sports gear, a green cap, and white canvas shoes. There he looks more like a Nigerian football official than a musical entertainer.

The women's dance group pair up in elegant attire looking like wives of rich lords in expensive white laces and costly beads to match. This show of opulence is suggestive of the great value Igbo women place on material achievements. They also don gorgeous head-ties of different colours and styles. Red head-scarfs and long wrappers tied to the chest distinguish the second group of *Lolo* (titled) women. Their shoulders are bare, revealing luxuriant healthy bodies. A white handkerchief can be seen on their hands with which they wave in rhythm to their dancing and wipe the sweat from their faces. As custodians of virtue, they must be bare footed so their feet are fully on earth. Waist movements are measured and controlled; hand gestures are also prominent.

Other male dancers wear white singlet and greatly prized dull red ("King) George" wrappers. They also wave the symbolic white handkerchief. Solo dances are common, occasionally providing for the dancer a chance to display own artistry. Amidst this group two clowns are seen; one bare-chested and tardy in his acts, the other severally dressed in casual sports jumpers or in singlet and jeans. Their asinine facial contortions and twisting movements are supposed to elicit amusement and laughter from the audience. Sometimes the scene will show a glimpse of the instruments of the *Ekpili* performance and their handlers. They are dressed in white tops and wrappers proudly beating their instruments. Occasionally we glimpse the guitars and piano and the range of musical drums and gongs *(ogene)* used in *Ekpe* dance performance. From the background they lend syncopated rhythms of Nigerian highlife music to the performance..

We are also left some remnants of traditional aesthetic in the ring composition that introduces the choral theme at the beginning of the performance. This allows for the exploration of more general sub-themes. The central and overriding idea, the futility and hopelessness of all things in this world, is supported with stories and satirical bouts at human behaviour. Sometimes the artiste combines his *Ekpili* with traditional story-telling entertainment called "akuko na egwu" (musical narrative). This also allows for an expatiation of motifs and dance patterns that finally return to the central theme in the chorus: the evilness of the world.

Chief Maduka's *Ekpili* version also comes with extensive application of traditional repetitive variations in song. The device of parallel lexical and syntactic structures is used generously and with a variation to the repetitious chorus. This choral is simple and memorisable and that is how Morocco's *Ekpili* grew in popularity among a broad spectrum of music lovers in Nigeria.

It may also be observed that the artistic vowelisation of Igbo phonemes "o" and "i" is utilised with great effect in the song. Recurring at the end of every line, there is a cadence and feeling of well-being they generate which enhance the popularity of his music:

Oyim Uba na Ese	My friend Uba,
nwa mama-o	beloved one
Jide ka iji-i	Hold fast to your gift
Jide kwa ka iji-o	Hold again to your gift
Oyim, jide kwa ka iji-i	My friend, hold fast to your gift
Ime elu me ala nwannem-o	What ever you do, my brother
Iilo na asiri ga dilili-i	Rancour and gossip must prevail.

This Igbo singer further offers a humour on modern marital relations to depict an abject money-loving, as against service-oriented society. Women are no longer traditional matriarchs of their household who work alongside their men-folks to raise children and maintain a robust barn. Now those marriage promises made during what they call "White wedding" seem valid as long as the economic considerations that bind them do not alter drastically. He supports this theme with a Hausa proverb interpreted thus:

When there's money then woman comes
When money goes, Oh, woman goes.

There are times when English language is used in the song to aim at comic relief or satire. An example is the popular refrain, "I love my darling", where the butt is on modern romance:

Nwanyi di ya nwelu ego,	The wife of a well-to-do husband
Ijuo ya kedu ka odi	When you ask how things are
Ife oga asi gi bu	She will answer you
"I love my darling	"I love my darling
"I love my darling,	I love my darling,
I love my darling.	I love my darling,
I love my darling,	my darling loves me
my darling loves me	So no circumstances
So no circumstances	can change my mind."
can change my mind."	

Sometimes in the performance the singer intersperses his Igbo with Nigerian Pidgin. The Pidgin, "abegi abegi", is his comic spoof at the offending Nigerian who would dare the Police at their own game of bribery and corruption.

Polisi jide onye dalu iwu	Police arrests a miscreant
Obido yowa Polisi	He starts to plead
"abegi abegi	"Oh please, Oh please
abegi abegi, abegi abegi."	please, please, please."

With songs and dances, the *Ekpiri* singer in a final gesture, reminds his audience of that traditional wisdom which emphasises that the world is like a mirror that reflects all the good and bad of one's actions to the doer:

Onye na-eme mma na-emelu onwe ya ma-o
N'alusi adi egbu mmadu na nkiti

Who does good deeds does so for himself
For Idol does not kill someone for naught.

Despite that African religion is being denigrated by the Christian word "alusi" (idol) for the gods, yet, behind the modern mask of religious bigotry among Igbo artistes lies a recognition of the ancient gods as impartial, punishing the wicked and rewarding the just eventually. In Morocco's *Ekpili* music this awareness is dulled by a new religious morality which holds society rotten and deviant from the will of a god who yet endows his chosen one in a mysterious way. He seems unaware that these imported religions and their arbitrary notions of a ruling tyrant and loving god rather corrupted the African universe in the first place. As the Igbo mind through the *Ekpili* singer counsels everyone to search his or her conscience, a code-mixing of language in English "check" and Igbo "-ibe" (suffix for continuing action) occurs in the fourth line of his verse:[18]

Onye ihuru na-aga kwulu kwulu kwulu
ijuo ya osi na oji ofo ga-ana
ma na ihem na-agwa umu uwa níme naijiria
Onye obuna *check*ibe onwe ye
Imara ma ogi so emebi naijiria-o
Nwannem n'uwa emebigo

When you see him milling with the crowd
Ask him and he says the just shall be free

> But what I tell you people of Nigeria
> Everybody check himself very well
> To find out if you are joining to spoil Nigeria
> My brother, the world is all so spoiled.

It may be presumed that general doubt and scepticism in moral and ethical life seem to be Igbo response to the vicious materialist cycle that grips their world all because Maduka's musical philosophy seems to thrive on a non-specific, noncommittal position between the wounded and despoilers of society with religion (God) as its symbolic centre. Where everyone must search his conscience to determine if one was part of the destroyers of a hostage nation, the artiste loses strength and focus on the urgency of communal cleansing, the invocation of Spiritual order, by which the Gods hitherto held the maintenance and adjudication of our affairs in their own delineated ways. And so by devolving resolution of cosmic balance to personal conscience, he replaces communal responsibility and group spiritual allegiance with modern Nigerian direction in selfish individualism.

Despite the foregoing, Chief Maduka is evidently an artiste in tune with the mind and character of his people, preferring not to use his art to sit in judgement over individuals and social tendencies but striving to mark a spot for himself as an artist to be reckoned with, at least, within his immediate cultural domain.

Ekpili music, no doubt, reveals unflattering patterns of modern Igbo mind, its spiritual conundrum in abject materialism and confusion of destiny. As a modern musical performance it also proves the argument among scholars that imitating Western precepts do not render the African arts with as much aesthetic and visionary fidelity as in the pure traditional performances.

Journal of New Poetry, 2009

B. Literature

5

And Tortoise flew...

Anezi Okoro. ***Flying Tortoise.***
Enugu: Delta Publications, 20004

The writing of Anezi Okoro is of major importance in the genre of children's literature in Africa. Few young readers of the seventies in Nigeria can easily forget the rascally child prodigy of the novel, *One Week one Trouble,* and his funny escapades in college. Wilson Tagbo's adventures in his new school were the delight of young boys and girls who saw in the boy hero the qualities of intelligence, wit, and bravery necessary for success in school and in life. Today these qualities have been subverted by Nigeria's military and civilian politicians. It now takes Western-type violence and mediocrity to take the highest political offices of a fifty year old nation.

Nevertheless the fictional rough diamond in many a character representation of the child hero like Anezi Okoro's Wilson Tagbo, and Nkem Nwankwo's Bayo Idowu in *Tales out of School*, has offered a rich cultural and intellectual service to young Nigerian readers. This is very much in the same manner that Achebe's Okonkwo story grew very real and large for every adult African reader of *Things Fall Apart*.

Such were the serial youth adventure stories that established a reputation for Okoro as one of the most entertaining and educating writers in Africa. He stands along with Cyprian Ekwensi, Onuora Nzekwu, and Nkem Nwankwo in this historic tradition of African story telling. Unfortunately while his larger work of adult short fiction, *Pariah Earth*, showcases an emerging tradition of African science fiction writing, Okoro's contribution to modern African writing has yet to be acknowledged by critics of the genre.

The publication in 2004 of *Flying Tortoise* by Anezi Okoro was yet another credit to the creative virtuosity of the septuagenarian writer for children. In twenty-six chapters, Okoro makes a fictional recreation of the tortoise legends in Igboland. For the first time in oral and written storytelling Tortoise leaves his terrestrial habitat to traverse outer space on a 'discovery mission'. In this book the tortoise of Igbo folk tales is transformed into a science-oriented tortoise who is equipped with high technological apparatuses and a super-scientific-mathematical mind. But more interesting is that this scientific-mind, science-wizard Tortoise still retains great traditional wisdom, unquenchable optimism and intellectual distinction. All these are added to his legendary reputation for tackling and confronting obstacles almost in the manner of fools who rush in where angels fear to tread.

Flying Tortoise importantly touches upon modern environmental problems. Tortoise's space probe is sparked by his apparent revulsion for human exploitation of the earth and environment. He had watched with horror as a gigantic Iroko is brought down by a sawing machine. Even more pathetic is the plight of ants, lizards and other smaller creatures that live in this tree. The impunity with which the flora and fauna of his homeland are devastated sparks off a protest which is underscored by his 'abandoning' earth for outer space. He explores space for life-alternatives in hopes of bringing over his wife, children and other animals if successful. To his chagrin Tortoise discovers that man has already invaded space with several satellites, probes and other exploration gadgets that litter there. Again he laments man's tardiness even in space. His adventure takes him through all the known planets.

Our legendary Tortoise comes back with the usual assumption that outer space is not ready yet to support other human life forms. But his temporary departure had created a furore as humans had monitored his progress through their space tracking gadgets. He returns to earth a hero. He reels out difficult puzzles for humans to decipher, the idea being to force them to recognise that animals have as much intelligence as humans. A sub plot develops around the theme of ethnic jealousies and rivalry which becomes more apparent as Tortoise's popularity grows.

Meanwhile some other animals interpret his fame as a threat to their own peaceful existence in the forests and they fear that tortoise, proud of his achievements, may begin to harbour ideas about dominating the affairs of the animal kingdom. As this disenchantment grows, divisions increase among them. Bigger animals are the most jealous. Finally, the animals organise themselves into two warring groups and fight a poorly matched war in which the smaller Lizard, Snail, Serpent, Ants, and Lightning defeat the bigger ones: Tiger, Elephant, Mongoose, Hare, Leopard, Eagle, etc. It is significant in mediation and conflict resolution efforts that the smaller animals employ their wit and cunning, rather than brawn, to defeat their larger opponents.

There may be the temptation to dismiss *Flying Tortoise* as a work of juvenile literature, especially with the tortoise character, yet when considered from the perspective of literature that makes significant observations on human nature and society, the book thrives as a fine study of life on earth. It is a parable of the folly, jealousy, avarice, ambition and all such positive (or negative) emotions that propel men and women either to their success or doom. Further, the story dramatizes Fanon's observations on the psychology of the oppressed. The animals had made some misleading assumptions and conclusions as to the cause(s) of their problems. They blame their own kind and seek the means of eliminating all but the real enemy. It takes a decisive confrontation, however, for them to identify their central adversary:

> Do we need another intervention from Lightning to make us accept … that we all belong to the animal kingdom. That our enemy cannot come from your side, nor your enemy from our side. That our true enemy… is man, not Super Tortoise. (174)

This awareness unites the animals as they plan a reception for Super Tortoise. The occasion provides them with the first opportunity to fight man on his own level by using their intelligence. The animals organise several puzzles through which they intend to reveal to man that they want to be treated with respect.

Notwithstanding that the highly scientific language, exposing the reader to a plethora of registers, makes *Flying Tortoise* a turgid read, but the employment of folk story tradition in modern literary narrative is a commendable attempt to preserve Igbo oral traditions and cultural heritage.

Anezi Okoro, no doubt, belongs to those rare Nigerian writers who have, in the words of his critic and interviewer,

> alter(ed) the future of our young for the better with works that appeal to and transform the restless and inquisitive mind of a child into an unquenchable thirst for knowledge, the use of which will reshape the future of our country… (Emezue 47-48).

Journal of African Literature and Culture, 2006

6

A Story of courage

Pauline K. Davids. *Opuliche*

AI: Handel Books, 2008

Although *Opuliche* was published only in the year 2002, its completion had taken place back in 1976 as the Davids manuscripts attest. Two whole decades and half had elapsed before its first publication and yet, as fiction, it was deemed necessary to protect the privacy of some people and communities as evident in the imaginary towns and villages in the novel: Ogu, Ndudi, Okpu, Nsu, etc. These contrast with actual places: Enugu, Nnobi and Aba south east Nigeria. There is also a mix of real and contrived names such as Angelina, Modiba, Dobendu, Mama Antoni, Venni, etc. The use of real and fictional names in the novel is significant as it allays the danger of discrepancy which can easily arise from the many cases of authorial opinions, judgments and cross narratives which abound in the story.

Then it is evident from the Davids narrative that Opuliche was a real person, if not the author of the story herself, raised in the gloomy times of colonial rule where missionary activities grappled with traditional ways of life. Ogu, the fictional birthplace of Opuliche, was understandably a society on the throes of change even as the people appeared steeped in traditional ways. Thus when Modiba is reported to have fallen back, dejected at her birth of the baby Opuliche, after the good neighbour, Ohuka, had replied to her question with the brusque exclamation: "It's a female" (14), we must not see the action as a future sign of poor parenting or the spite of a wicked neighbour. On the contrary we are ready for the contrast of traditional opinion and behaviours with the positive capabilities of the girl hero who has just come.

Davids divides her novel in two parts, each containing short episodic chapters and incidents that inspire compulsive reading. Part One, containing a prologue and eleven chapters, shows Opuliche's birth and her early upbringing by her parents, Modiba and Dobendu. Although both parents had wanted a male child, Opuliche is fervently loved and cared for. As usual in traditional societies, the maternal presence looms large; it is the guide and strict disciplinary influence on youngsters, male and female. Through Modiba, the young Opuliche is to adopt the resilient and determined attitude that will see her through her many struggles. And with her sudden exit from the world, our Opuliche is to learn the ropes through some hard personal decisions that she had imbibed from her mother.

Part Two, also comprising eleven chapters, further chronicles Opuliche's travails through school. In fact the entire Opuliche story seems to be the ordeals and struggles of a young woman to acquire education. Modiba's early death in the first section is closely followed by Dobendu's transition in the second part of the story. This is rendered by the author in a manner that heightens the tragic dimension of Opuliche's life. With the death of her father Opuliche's travails are further worsened by penury and frustrations with college authorities.

Opuliche's school adventures, which her story truly encapsulates, are told by Davids with quaint, illustrative details that evoke memories of austere, provincial lifestyles:

> The town of Ogu was made up of several villages including Ogu and Ndudi. Ndudi on the opposite side was a forest village shielded with large baobab trees....The general belief in Ndudi was that the next-door neighbour must be out to undo one's own family. So the watchword was always 'beware never befriend.' (22)

Here, tradition is evidently the hard but disciplined way and must either blend with the tenuous demands of missionary education and modern livelihood or entirely give way to them. The author is hardly on the side of any of the modern or traditional life ways. Rather she is a commentator on a history of personal struggles. What conclusions we derive from her many censures – as in the criticism of convent traditions, the inferiority complex of 'holy Nweje' girls, or Opuliche's killing of the sacred snake – can only seem obvious from our own intense reading and response to the story. Davids is particularly successful in the exposition of traditional and colonial flaws in a way that often reveals her strong capacity for liberated thinking:

> The few girls who had been in the convent for some years often threatened the new boys' school girls with severe punishment from the sisters because of their rawness and lack of manners. 'You're very rude,' they would complain.
> 'You have no manners Opuliche,' the reformed, tame and polished girls would reprimand her. 'Can't you say please?'
> Opuliche will hear this scolding ten times in an hour. She would watch the tame girls twist their mouths in distaste. (57)

While her omniscient narrative style allows for authorial interjections and explanations that characterise most biographical narratives, the story teller also shows some craft in handling these comments to the overall didactic purpose of her story:

> This convent type of celibacy was brought from outside Africa. It was a strange notion that bred many desperate and unhappy women. At the end those relatives that she had trained usually despised the 'holy nweje' girl. They would even make fun of her single status. They would shun her in her old age. At this point, the holy nweje girl could be any thing but happy. Children were so important in the life of the average woman that a woman could be mother of her children without being married. However, Holy Nweje wouldn't know until they got to the dead end. What a fix for the proud, good and holy nweje girl! (95)

Today's college girls and boys will be fascinated to read Opuliche's struggle to acquire education in those years. Her embarrassing fall while returning from a local stream at Adazi, with her bucket trailing her descent down the hill, reminds us of series of similar events in real life accounts. When she ate a whole pot of rice all alone in the night, only to demand from Celibret a few hours later who did this to her, she was acting out a familiar chapter in our own youths when we found consolation in our favourite meals. For some of us, it was *eba* and vegetable soup and we could never stop eating this delicacy. One colleague in my school days, who must not be named here, had written a whole poem which stated that when he saw a cow eating grass he would immediately think of *Afang* soup!

There are several more serious chapters on Opuliche's growth and development. The burial of her father in her absence and her lone fight against this practice that disregards the female member of the household are two cases that draw our sympathy firmly on the side of the heroine. No doubt there is always the compulsion of reading Feminist theories in novels by African women writers, especially where traditional practices are sorely criticised, but there are other important insights to the Opuliche story. For example, the comments on some missionary sisters in this book is an indictment of their religion and its proselytising mission in Africa. This may seem to justify later Nigerian government decision to take over the running of missionary schools at the time. Incidents of the prejudice and bigotry of some reverend sisters or the strange morality of 'holy Nweje' girls form important sub themes of the novel. These are aspects of colonial mentality inhered in African nation states. Reading Opuliche's and her friends' experiences, one is tempted to wonder if the blind zealotry fed by religious education should always be swallowed with no second thought. In other words, how much of our 'common sense' - which by the way is not common, as a famed teacher would say - must we suspend in the name of religious or any political followership for that matter? This, too, is another significant sidebar to the Davids story.

We have to follow the child hero as she traverses the stage of innocence only to be launched unceremoniously into adulthood and its travails. We join to laugh at her follies and tend to cry with her as she grapples with her many frustrations and disappointments. All these are told in rapid and mingled succession of events and thoughts. It is remarkable that *Opuliche* has such a quick narrative pace; thus a whole life account is rendered in just over one hundred pages. Where other writers would fill tons of epic details, Davids cuts through unnecessary hagiographic tedium and compresses her narration. The result is a compact life account of twenty-two short chapters whose prologue deigns to introduce a story of female child discrimination while the entire story achieves the opposite effect of female triumph and achievement.

The epilogue bears witness to a most revolutionary redefinition of self from one of acquiescence to tradition and custom to the firm belief in one's intuition and sense of familial identity. In rejecting discriminatory practices by religious denominations and also our traditional endorsement of those often mistaken oracular proclamations on our destiny, Davids shows us that we men or women, like Opuliche, are really the ones in control of our beliefs and, thenceforth, our destiny:

> From that day, Opuliche started to think that this woman, who used to get the 'truth' from the oracle, must have not been a good friend of Mohiba. 'Otherwise, why should the oracle say that the son was my father while this next one was not my mother? Perhaps the problem was with the oracle,' she summed it all up.
>
> So in baptising the child, Opuliche called her Modiba. The name Modiba, added to the child's first name, was to honour Opuliche's mother. To her, the little baby girl was Modiba and no other. The woman she had known and loved for but some brief time in her life had every reason to return to her. (137)

With her children named after the two most important people in her life: father and mother, Opuliche leaves us with the proverbial wisdom of the triumph of all good things over challenges of fate and circumstance. Thus whether explicit or subtly contrived in the actions of Davids' girl character, the discerning reader is sure to glean a few gems of wisdom from the adventures of Opuliche. These are no doubt cut from the larger cloak of experience with which this remarkable writer invokes the theme of female educational empowerment with self assurance.

Pauline Davids' female creation may well represent the classic heroine of modern African writing. It is the story of every woman who must struggle through an old tradition of boy-child preference. From conception and its attendant worries for a male child, through birth and training, the African woman has squarely faced what seems a man's world with its benign disregard for the girl child. Here is one who struggles to overcome the obvious disadvantages of being born and raised in a patriarchal male-conditioned society. Her courage and triumph in the face of all odds should be the hope of all women of character this side of the world.

Opuliche, Introduction, 2008

7

Teacher's art

Joy. M. Etiowo. *Mma and other poems*
Lagos: Handel Books, 2006

IN her maiden volume entitled *Mma Collection,* Nigerian scholar, Joy Etiowo, presents 27 poems that anchor upon the sensitivity of those I have called the younger generation of African poets some of whose works strike us for the lyrical, clear and unaffected expression in art.

Mma begins on a trepid note, taking on the subject matter of poetry and testifying to its dampening impact on the poet's feeble sensitivity at the early encounter. It brings forth my favourite image of a bather on a cold harmattan morning by the side of the local stream trembling and fearful of the initial plunge:

Your rhythms frightened me

And your rhymes stiffened my nerves
You made a rumbling in me
At every point of our contact. (13)

Etiowo encapsulates the sublime triumph of essence over precept at this first phase of meeting when the confusion that 'frighten(s)' and 'stiffen(s) our nerves becomes, much later with the bold plunge into its depths, 'a nourishment' of self and a 'discovery' of channels of imaginative 'assemblage of words'.

Today you are the channel
Of my imagination
You are the tinder
That ignites in me
A burning passion for assemblage of words. (13)

In a universal sense *Mma* may stand as a tribute to sublime creation to which a soul stands on 'bended knees' humble and submissive before the maker of all things.

You are the ground under my feet
You are the comfort under my knees
In the valley you lift me high
On the mountains make me a haven. (34)

Likewise it marks a personal note of dedication to many years of fruitful experience – this to the major inspirer of Etiowo's verse: the great 'Mma Teacher' herself. It is to her that

The chalk and the board

Scrubbed with charcoal and herbs
Shine in its blackness. (24)

The honour extends to other 'hero(es)' whose legacies prod us to reflect upon their courageous lives, and even savour the natural feelings of loss consequent upon our final separation from them:

You are mother of great kings
And men who trod the land
Obol Omini Bassey... (35)

Etiowo's Mma poems may succeed not so much by intent to correct perceived anomies as the deeper need to recognise aesthetic and cognitive responsibilities of individuals and community. Touching communal base, as evidenced by these poems, does not exclude in its sweep reminders about our social or political environment. Nigeria has offered the poetess the particularity from which wider dimensions of our existence can be assessed and revolved. For example, when we are reminded of the three Rs in 'The Cry' we recognize this is one part of our national monuments of 'dreams destroyed':

Thirty five years have gone
There are still the cries
Of fathers killed
Of mothers laid
Of children stolen
Of property leased. (17)

But as the product of the visioning is not desensitised in bashful memories, there is a balance of feeling which gives satisfaction that our poetry can be as temperate as 'we decry/ ...our (myriad) obsession(s)'. Thus even as

> ...dogs have their meals
> in silver plates
> ...
>
> And humans beg
> For unequal portion (15)

we can also celebrate friends that wipe our 'tears of lust and pain / sharing (our) mat of sorrow.' We can even dedicate our hearts to icons like Inah-Aki, Onen-Joshua, Ikpi-Willie and the great Mma herself, mother of not just one, but all those whose paths had crossed with hers in the course her exemplary life.

I am quite convinced in the potential of poetry of the younger generation. Ours, like I stated elsewhere, comes through with greater feeling and is not enmeshed, as earlier poets did, in pursuits of differing grand, intellectual, opus dei of their schools. There is the romanticism–if the appellation can be allowed–inherent from the continuing resolution in emotive responses over the dispassionate intellect that often beclouds the ingenuity of art which deigns to take the finesse of artistic distancing in poetry with more than its deserved pinch of salt. Thus the morale that can be found in Etiowo's collection is for African poetry to return to its ancient purpose as a deeply involved and pleasurable creative reflection for the modern-day griot and her listeners.

Mma and other Poems, Introduction, 2006

8

Close strangers

Judith Lutge Coullie (ed). *The Closest of Strangers: South African Women's Writing*

LaJohannesburg: Witts University Press, 2004

JUDITH Coullie's book, *The Closest of Strangers*, attempts to portray the intricate relationships that lend meaning to the term 'existence' and 'womanhood' in South Africa. In her statement of objective Coullie acknowledges the essence of all attempts at the great works:

> My hope is that these extracts may teach us how to transcend our own narrow concerns and engage with experiences and truths that may differ from our own, even though such imaginative engagement can only be partial, fragmentary and crude. (3)

The book has nine sections, with each section spanning none to ten years of history. Its merit lies in its concentration on stories that denote the 'human angle' to South Africa's frightful history of apartheid and violence. It yields to us the travails of women during the turmoil and turbulence that South Africa had passed through. That the stories and poems are culled from actual biographies, autobiographies and interviews gives the impression of participation on the part of the reader. It feels that one is getting the story directly from the narrator and lends an aura of truth to these experiences. From that perspective too, the Izibongo(s) (personal/oral praises panegyrics) appear to be appropriately situated within the context of the work. With regard to South Africa's history and its implication for the citizens, Lyndall Gordon in her introduction to the book cites Historian Cherryl Walker as noting that:

> [W]omen's sense of community with other women, the basis of their perception of themselves ... was circumscribed by sturdy boundaries of language, ethnicity and the broader race consciousness around which South African society was organized. (1)

Most of the stories (save few) tend to justify this assertion. They seem to reflect the "... paradox of ubiquitous racism ... (which) branded all South Africans, in a sense binding them together in their experiences... of the extremes of segregation" (3).

It might appear a little hasty to conclude that the story of South Africa is only that of violence yet each of the nine sections in this anthology reveals the vicious strings that run through the whole South African debacle. From wars, lynching, mob killings, incarceration, police molestation and forced evictions, through rape, thefts, escapes, forced labour, spurned or thwarted love and family separations, the lives of South African women chronicle two centuries of violence. Projecting from the consciousness of the victims or 'victim witnesses,' the nightmarish tales adjust the lens of reality to reveal the universal humanity beneath the events. Possibly this is one of the editorial objectives of this compilation. The first section is entitled 'The Birth of South Africa'. The stories detail the bloodbath that preceded the birth of South Africa during the Anglo-Boer wars. Sarah Raal chronicles the many dangers she faced fighting alongside men in the war. The general picture conveyed is that the women suffered and were exposed to even greater dangers than their men during the wars.

'Unions and Divisions' contains four stories out of which only one (Prue Smith's) appears to have relevance to the underlying theme of British racism after the Anglo-Boer wars. The sum is that racial discrimination was meted out to non-British nationals including the Dutch. Although this section is preceded by a good introduction, the stories that appear here do not lend it much structural cohesion. Perhaps more stories directly concerned with the basic expositions of the introduction should have featured here to achieve the unity of vision.

Prue Smith's account might be seen as a white woman's reaction to entrenched racial segregation that had favoured her kind. In contrast, she forges emotional alliance with her black nurse upon whom she had depended. Although the story comes to us from Smith's white viewpoint, yet her revelation that the maid's baby was named after her seems to underscore the mutual emotional dependence of two human beings irrespective of the divisions of the society. Mgqwetho's Izibongo in this section has very little relevance with the objective. Perhaps its inclusion is simply justified by the period of its production.

'Enfranchisement and Disenfranchisement' chronicles events that happened between 1930 and 1940. This was the period of great political upheaval especially for blacks and Asians singled for racist victimisation around this period. Then the main opposing political party, the Communist Party, enjoyed much popularity. It was a period of great trial for this party as its tenets and practices were put to severe test. One of such tests is that of the relationships between different racial groups. This is illustrated in Pauline Podbrey's story of the love between herself and her Indian husband. That this story appears in 'Foundations of Apartheid' seems to render the structural divisions unnecessary. Indeed, save some few cases, many of the stories would have conveniently appeared as one major section. For instance the stories in 'Enfranchisement' and 'Foundations of Apartheid' could have conveniently featured as one section with 'Apartheid Escalates' or 'Winds of Repression.'

The preoccupation with 'violence' in the stories notwithstanding there still appear some ideas of positive dimensions.

While Dr. Goonam's experience in 'Enfranchisement...' captures prevalent gender prejudices, dichotomies and challenges, Katie Makanya's account of her job experience with

Dr. McCord reveals, like Prue Smith, that love, loyalty and dedication transcend the racial boundary. In this guise, Charlene Smith's story of rape, and even more importantly, her 'liberated' awareness which guides her report of the incidence, reveal a quality of awareness that attempts to transcend the confines of environment. Her report admits of success in overcoming racial biases which seem to dictate and muddle our perception of reality. It is significant that her report details a cognisance that insight that although raped by a black man, there lies a deeper understanding of the human nature that drives our predictable reactions:

> I cry, "I'm terribly sorry, but he raped me. I don't have my clothes with me".
> My white neighbour goes to fetch his wife. My black neighbour leads me gently away.
> "Please cut off this masking tape. I can't move properly." I try to move my bloodied hand. My black neighbour gets something and with the greatest gentleness cuts off the masking tape and frees my hand.

After this report she justifies why she has to reveal the racial identity of her neighbours who played a significant palliative role in her trauma. She states:

> I tell you the race of my neighbours because I want you to know that rape is not about race, as some South Africans think. It is not about what men do. It is about what a few sick individuals do. It has nothing to do with race or malehood. Indeed, for most part men treated me better than women that

night. (368)

With her exceptional depth of perception and spiritual awareness Smith's traumatic tale, reported in *The New South Africa*, almost flattens the ironical and sad twist of her experience. Her higher awareness would readily lend an insight to forging the dream of the new South Africa while her message of hope simply proclaims that people need to cross gender and racial boundaries in order to develop the human potential. Smith's report appears to highlight the view that life and existence in the new South Africa can only be achieved when people have a greater understanding of their neighbours (at work, home, or in the community) some of whom had been their closest strangers in the past.

One way of achieving this insight appears to be the objective of this anthology. With decades of political, cultural and economic divide officially dismantled in South Africa, individuals are challenged to eschew emotional and psychological mind-sets by availing themselves of the opportunity being offered to synergise others' experiences.

It must be observed that the 'Izibongo' oral poems do not communicate much of message or art. Their scant yield in meaning and poetic virtuosity may be attributed to the brevity of their presentation. Again some of the stories coming as autobiographies have the ring of contrivance. A good example is Winnie Mandela's account of her early relationship with her husband which may have been constructed to suit some simply emotional or post traumatic purpose.

Judith Coullie's anthology could however be enriched with the experiences of more black women writers in a subsequent edition.

Journal of African Literature and Culture, 2006

9

Some ending narratives

Bettina Weiss (ed). The End of Unheard Narratives: *Contemporary Perspectives on Southern African Literature*

Heidelberg: Kalliope Paperbacks, 2004

IN her introduction to *The End of Unheard Narratives* Bettina Weiss puts forward the proposition that the title signifies that 'former(ly) unheard narratives' have 'receive(d) a powerful expression' and have by the book publication 'cease(d) to remain in the closet'. The intent on giving voice to the 'marginal' or 'minority' voices achieves a congenial purpose of reappraising the philosophical and socio-political imperatives which give impetus to 'silencing narratives' deemed 'unpleasant' or even 'dangerous'.

This book diligently identifies such narratives as those dwelling on themes of homosexuality, HIV/AIDS, prostitution and sexual exploitation, and all the stigmatised peoples of these categories 'who struggle for acceptance and humanity'.

Consequently the essays are commendable for their promise of giving 'an enlarged and enlightening insight' although the major entries become, for the first and second parts, a consolidation of fringe and 'abject' subject matters replete with their complex intrigues and oppositions all plodding vicariously along the familiar path of gender and social conflicts inscribed by Feminist movements that blew across Europe and the rest of the world.

Annemarie van Niekerk's 'A Leaking Categories' featuring an autobiographical work *Rachel, Woman of the Night* by a South African sex worker, Rachael Lindsay, who explores the inside prism of 'the oldest trade in the world' makes a befitting introduction to the hardy objective of authenticating the 'Other', particularly as the subject of prostitution had hitherto been neglected in major literary materials of the bio- and auto-biographical kinds. Niekerk's highlight of the entry of South African literature to the discourse on topic of prostitution is treated with notable objectivity and scholarship which seeks to identify with the protagonist's point of view to commend neither censure nor opprobrium. This capacity for objectification of the literary material in critical studies, as against intensely opinionated and dominantly theoretical prejudice, is the much needed approach to African literature even as the fad of 'talking back' and 'writing back' has engaged many theorists of postcolonial literatures. In Berveley Dube's review, 'Re-Imagining the Prostitute in Society: A Critique of the Male Writer's Perspective in Zimbabwean Literature', this shows a pattern where early prejudices against minority opinions seem to be giving way to a less subjective, more sympathetic attitude on the part of writers of fiction.

Lizzy Attree's paper, 'Reshaping Communities: The Representation of HIV/AIDS in Literature from South Africa and Zimbabwe', surveys different perspectives on the AIDS pandemic that has ravaged Southern African nations, dutifully ferreting out attempts at the re-inscriptions of Africa as a dark continent with the devastation (not excluding the myths and ignorance surrounding it) of exploited, poverty stricken African communities. However, the study ignores to present indigenous alternatives to modern transitions in the post colonial history of Africa's exploitation, an indication of the extent of amnesia in modern Southern African academics about the overarching importance of the indigenous heritage, and thereby of history beyond apartheid and postcoloniality. The result is that the new South African amalgam of racial attitudes in the region might have formulated another typecast of sorts bordering on the main-other, persecutor-victim divide which is not mitigated by the shallow blaming of 'homophobic attitudes' and 'patriarchal power relations' for the silencing of some of the world's 'minority' sexual expressions today.

Part II 'Voicing Tough Facts and Gentle Suggestions' appears a redundant sectionalising of clearly homogenous materials as the two remarkable works of Tom Odhiambo: 'Socio Sexual Experiences of Black South African Men' and Bettina Weiss: 'Approach to Homoerotic Female Desire' may well have functioned in 'Abject Bodies'. This may also apply to Robert

Mupond's 'The Eyes of a Buck: Fighting the Child in Zimbabwean Short Story in English' editorially figured in 'tough facts/ gentle suggestions' for the writer's treatment of the child figure in literature, an approach that reexamines held assumptions which the writer confronts at the beginning of his essay i.e., of children being, in Leslie Fiedler's words, 'symbols of offended innocence' especially in the creative writings of 'frontline' nation states as has been the histories of the Southern (and other) African nations.

Three papers by Katrin Berndt ('Eloquent Silence as a Mode of Identity'), Margie Orford ('Transition, Trauma and Triumph: Contemporary Namibian Women's Literature') and the duo of Dorothy Driver and Meg Samuelson ('History's Intimate Visions: Yvonne Vera's The Stone Virgins') form the third part of the book tagged Re(N)egotiating and Restoring Identities. Of these three, Katrin Berndt's 'Eloquent Silence' takes the arguable position that the silence of the female protagonist can be 'eloquent' and (for Berndt) provides an opening ('interstice') for expressing so-called 'subaltern approaches' for truthfulness as against the lies of official historiographies on Southern African movement and progress.

Yet there is something ultimately distasteful for its racist assumptions in Berndt's idea (unabashedly Spivak's) of the 'lack of expressive and narrative power of inferior group'. The author's argument deliberately replete with superficial postcolonial theories of 'subjective' and 'objective' approaches to truthfulness reinforces outmoded hegemonic myths and fallacies and appropriates to itself the same language and definitions of untoward inscriptions which function to the detriment of the victims of colonialism's entrenched interests such as the Southern Africa of their study. These give the perspectives coming from *The End of Unheard Narratives* a tendency to further recast the alienation of those 'abject' conditions and not their integration in serious literary or philosophical preoccupation. Here again one wonders at the editor's position that 'prostitutes and women voices were/are silenced...for the purposes of 'creating controversial moral values', especially where the main historical conveyors of these morality and attitudes have been Western /Hebraic-Christian civilisation and its theories of world history, human existence, racial, family or sex relations – the last of which Southern African literatures have lately been identified as 'individualising' or particularising upon.

This important historical insight is lost on the contributors, with the exception of Odhiambo who mentions, only partially, that 'Christianity emphasised heterosexuality and condemned homoerotic practices', thereby aiding our argument that the redoubtable legacies of the West lie behind the world's most noxious sickness of bigotry, conquest and domination of the perceived Other. Yet Odhiambo in his paper asserts rather lamely that 'many African societies have had alternate sex practices for ages' without evident basis for that claim. Similarly Bettina Weiss declares that 'this so-called un-Africanness (of lesbianism and homosexuality) was/is not that un-African at all (119), all in gallant efforts to subvert the anti-homoerotic rhetoric. This is where the idea of contextual/literary frameworks of artistic interpretations clogs observations on the larger merits of creative works. It marks an academic tendency to stultify literature with a stricture complex in which many a generation of critical studies can be trapped for longer, deficient periods of the rest of its history.

One is however optimistic that with the end of apartheid and the so-called political literature produced by its mixed black, white, and coloured populace all that the new 'individual' themes have to offer are not entirely riveted on counteracting or propagating fringe subject matters which the first through the third parts of this study have done. Thus the last part, 'The Past a Mediator for the Present' marks a significant stirring of awareness in Southern African literature as Agnes Murungi's 'The Invention of (Oral) Tradition and the Imagining of a New Nation' shows of Ellen Kuzwayi's *Sit Down and Listen* collection of stories. Murungi harmonises the notion of tradition and modernity as separate concepts. Her idea of a 'useable past', drawing a relevant note from the cerebral Lewis Nkosi whose interactions with other African writers of his times highlight this effort, serves, in Murungi's excellent phrase, 'to recognise a South African identity that is based on a deeper sense of cultural retrieval'.

This negotiation of a tenuous trado-modern divide witnesses a wider experimentation with the form and style of narrative involving established and popular traditions of black (and other non-black) culture(s). Agnes Murungi's study and Jessica Henry's '"How All Life Is Lived in Patches": Quilting Metaphors in the Fiction of Yvonne Vera' are therefore the watershed in these contemporary perspectives on Southern African literary aesthetics mainly for their departure from the preoccupation with aesthetically stymied symptoms of adolescent psychosis and sex/ gender violence replete in the celebrated literatures of the Southern African region.

As a work which in the editor's promise 'hold(s) the potential to subvert and destabilise rigid conceptions' this objective, it must be conceded, has been swiftly executed with just twelve critical submissions for which Weiss must be commended. It is a step in the right direction as it contributes eloquently to the discourse toward eliminating all manners of prejudice, violence and discrimination that have tainted the human race all through its slow and tortuous civilisations. Sustaining this burden of self and collective redemption from past and present entrapments certainly involves concentrated, deeper, and more original insights on the part of Southern African scholars and writers.

Journal of African Literature and Culture, 2006

C. Chat

10

Critics of the new poetry

Literary Chat (with GMT Emezue)

GMT: I am pleased to have you on Literary Chat Forum. The theme of this debut, 'Critics of the New Poetry', is borne from concerns about the role of literary critics in the development of Nigerian poetry of our generation. With volumes of poetry and fiction to your credit, I believe you can comment on Nigerian poetry in earnest. What is your opinion about the simple poems that have characterised Nigerian poetry in the past thirty years after the war?

CE: Thank you for the theme on the new poetry - being the recent voices that have come out of Nigerian civil war experience and Nigerian politics of nation building (or nation breaking, more appropriately). My opinion is that the new poetry cannot help being simple and concerned with social problems or political issues and that even in other cultures, you notice that poetry has tended to this direction too. The era of poetry woven with fusions of Latin and Greco-Roman myths has gone. The point I like to raise is how the new poet has complemented his/her role within traditional heritage and modern challenges that stare him in the face.

GMT: Many are of the opinion that the traditional artiste in Africa has roles in the society, identifiable roles among which is to shape, teach, instruct, criticise and direct, for the reason that he lives and moves among his people and is very much part of whatever they are doing. And it is the duty of the critic of new Nigerian poetry to espouse in a forum like this how the new poetry has fared, what direction they think the new role should take. Unfortunately it seems the kind of education we are given makes us the more educated we are, the more ineffective.

CE: In other words, what can the critic do about our writing? As you rightly observed, the greater problem lies with you members of the Ivory Tower who can barely sieve the wheat from the chaff if you permit the cliche. Instead we have seen critics presenting a doggerel as the high point of art. He is full of praises because they are written by the teacher who supervised his graduating essay or his tribesman and the contradictions between his glowing encomiums for the work and the excerpts we see do not convince anyone. So critics seem to have lacked adequate interpretation of values. They are custodians of the scholarly enterprise that may later feature good reference points in literary studies. If they are afraid, if they shun or shrink from the *bolekaja* dialectics, at least, they should offer some better alternative. What makes for good literature? Beside merely enumeration of metaphors and similes what can we find that enrich the corpus?

GMT: I agree that there is a big job for critics of the new poetry. The avalanche of poems inundating readers regularly from the print are rude anti-climaxes. And the tragedy is that our scholars can no longer distinguish good from bad. Because these scholars are on a payroll, many of these poets are their patrons either as teachers or political friends and associates from whom they expect some favour, so the critics praise these writers, thereby misleading younger readers. But the artiste in Africa had a traditional role which he has lately compromised. He used to make sure that he directs, instructs and does not care whose feet he steps on. He sees his role as a duty and attends to it with an almost divine devotion. In local parlance, he 'does not look at anybody's face' while performing this task. Our poets, especially the good ones, have taken on this role even better. Other times the problem is not so much with poets as with critics who are not doing much job. At the best what many offer are merely interpretations of poems. 'The poet says this and that.' but this is just the elementary part. And it is time we were done with western terminologies because we have our yardsticks.

The practice of merely enunciating the parts and functions of poetry is elementary and criticism should go beyond this to evolve further critical standards of our own. There are other yardsticks from around the world. There is eco-criticism, quite recently. Deconstruction was there and died for want of relevance. But I know that in the African system we have yardsticks and standards which the critics only need to apply. The critic of new Nigerian poetry needs to be conversant with some of these standards which are reflections of African philosophy. Yes, one should interpret but one should also tally with tradition so that those who are interested in writing will not fall into the trap of our predecessors either in too much borrowing or ineffectual assimilation of critical notions. It is good to borrow, but when one borrows to the point of losing identity that is where the problem lies.

CE: Indeed this is what makes your efforts commendable being the truly first concentration of critical journal effort in a particular phase of writing and on a particular genre of literature: poetry. This is really nice and you should have the support of every poet and writer any day. I too have often wondered what it is that makes Nigerian poetry so different from the non poetry disciplines as to warrant very little concentration in terms of works done in this area.

GMT: It was necessary we put up this effort because in the non-poetry disciplines like drama and prose there have been some work in those areas. In fact they are always viewed as a familiar terrain. So you find that for a critic of the novel he doesn't have to beat about the bush. There are models for him to emulate both in Europe and Africa but for the critic of Nigerian poetry, it is doubtful. For instance, with the older critics like Echeruo and Nwoga, you discover that these scholars saw their job as midwives or interpreters. The poets of that generation are conveniently called second generation poets. For those in that group: Soyinka, Clark, Uka and Okigbo, you find that critics felt they had a job to do there because these poets wrote in ways that created a problem for the average reader. But with the new poetry the reverse seems to be the case. Ideas are well known; issues that affect the masses are all familiar. Their English is not of that turgid formal diction. Some have even explored the pidgin although with very little following or audience. But the idea of domestication has really caught on and the language had undergone serious developments. You find that for the critic it is not interpreting what the poem is saying that only counts because almost anyone can give you an idea what is being said.

CE: Yes. And this has also aided the density of praises, the encomiums. Most reviews of poetry today can barely show some objectivity about the prosaic lines, the unimaginative and ludicrous assertions of protest that have completely characterised the idea of new poetry. We do not see your critics honestly showing the limitations of such works which would otherwise have motivated our writers to be studious and more artistically effective. So I believe that criticism of poetry in

Nigerian communities has stultified for the fact that it is becoming another panegyric of its own. If we could identify salient features in a work of art, showing its strong points and weak elements, we will go a long way in critical studies of African or Nigerian poetry.

GMT: Let me move this chat further and ask in what language does the new Nigerian poet create? I think that this is a very important question in that it will help our critics to understand what the poet is actually saying and how he says it. For me, many of these new Nigerian poets tend to create in indigenous languages. A few years ago, I had the opportunity to talk with two younger poets and put this question to them: How and in what language do they create? Although both of them are from culturally different areas of Nigeria, but they gave me the same reply – that they create in their indigenous languages.

So you find that for these poets, the ideas first mature in indigenous language and concepts they are familiar with, then turn into English or they look about for English language equivalents for some of the things they already have. So you find out that in their poetry, they don't have deliberate similes and rhyming patterns, the type we encounter in European poetry. Their models are often the traditional artistes. And because their creative view is filled with what they already know traditionally, not what they were taught in school, they begin to translate these into English language and we now encounter some language code-switching and all that. Because when they do not find a good English language equivalent, they transport that same idea directly into the local language or, sometimes, they try to make poor translations of it. This is usually done on purpose. So for you to understand the poem you need to retranslate it or take it back to the indigenous language in order to get the beauty and skill.

CE: Well, speaking as a poet here, I do not think in Igbo and then write in English. I am confronted with the creative process as a communication that goes beyond language and visualise an interaction that goes towards the inner dimensions of the individual. And that interaction can neither be solely imagistic nor entirely symbolic; in other words, the interaction transcends the boundaries of language. It is a knowingness which goes so deep within the individual that the problem comes in lending expression to this knowingness, to this self instinctual understanding or realisation. That problem comes when you want to give verbal expression to this experience within the individual. I believe that the verbal expression is limited in any language it chooses; it can give vent neither to very deep feelings nor the depth of realisation that I am trying to make. But I am left with no other choice. I have to communicate through that language given me, being English. And I make haste to state that even the best mind faced with this realisation discovers that the activity of expression through language is inadequate to communicate the profundity and intensity of experience.

That is speaking on the individual plane. There is no doubt that some poets could claim to think first in their indigenous languages. I would rather prefer the allusions and subtle expressions that come with some of Ushie's poems and the individualised thoughts that are borne from intense personal experience which I find in Adewale. Onwudinjo's vividness and clarity give dramatic impetus to his *Women of Biafra* collections. His war poems are clearly action poems. These are younger poets of my generation. But where the individual is always confronted with translating, thinking in original language and expressing that original language into another language being English gives us a large room for deviation; we go wide of the mark in understanding the creative process. The poetic expression for me essentially is an attempt to reach wider levels of meanings, wider spheres of understanding. The language the individual chooses to express it is entirely up to him but he should communicate in such a way that he offers the reader, the audience, an ability to understand that experience. If he becomes irrelevant like the early poetry, he will completely lose his audience. If he succeeds, all well and good; he has helped to expand their understanding. He has conscripted, so to say, other beings into the landscape of his visioning. And I think that is where the success of a work of art lies.

GMT: Yes, but I also feel that in terms of creativity, perhaps, just perhaps (I am not much of a poet anyway) the subject matter, and the language that the poet is dealing with actually affects his outlook. In your poems, your anthology, *African Eclipse* for instance, most of the issues are on the social plank. You discover that, or I may say…it is not just an idea that you are trying to project – the idea of the individual finding the self. Well, it might be there, but in this case, it is totally subsumed with your concern for society. So I detect that even your language there shows a marked change when compared with your other *Full Moon*. There I should say that there are lots of private sentiments and the language changes too. With *African Eclipse*, the language there borders on the communal, the traditional African that we are talking about. For instance, you made use of the oracle medium, the African idea of divination in the poem you entitled 'Oracle'. And in those that deal on contemporary issues, your language there is overwhelmed with political registers and images. So I will like to say that probably, once the creative process has emerged through the individual, the next concern based on the idea the poet is espousing might be what language to convey. I think that's where *African Eclipse* serves the same purpose and reflects the same concerns of the new poetry.

So *Full Moon* is overly concerned with the individual, and the individual's ability to rise above limiting circumstances, and what makes it new poetry, I think, is its lyrical nature. And in terms of celebrating the self, *Full Moon* has a lot in common with (Toyin Adewale's) *Naked Testimonies*. Both poetry show an overly concern with self and similar use of language.

CE: Yes, but don't forget we are talking about the language of poetry and creativity inhered there. I doubt not that having started writing in a our generation one would say that the works belong in the mode of new Nigerian writing, but not in the sense of your presumed manners of expression. I do not consciously seek to write within a particular language choice or imagery so that I would be considered a new Nigerian poet. As a writer I look at – just as you said – use of appropriate diction and expressions to highlight the message. I might have explored the opening motif of the diviner in the 'Oracle' stanzas, and you can rightly say there are overt vilification of some historical personalities in *African Eclipse*, that is true. But I did not think in any mother tongue and later then translated, or employed some code-switching, in order to qualify as new Nigerian poet. You see, this thinking in mother-tongue might evolve a stereotype that we cannot grow out of in a long time.

I recognise the fact that individuals could also form their own approach and the writer or critic of poetry holds the onus of these subtle differences in art. I have read a lot of critical works on so called new Nigerian poetry and they all seem to say the same thing. You recently, in a previous publication, (ALJ B5) complained about this trend in Nigerian movie industry. I think it was Ossie Enekwe there who said that because the artistes and critics have abandoned their calling the charlatans had to take over so that what you find in the industry is a stupid, repetitive stereotype that has portrayed a very bad image of the country. Don't you think that today we stand to have a stereotype new Nigerian poetry where your literary scholars are overwhelmed by issues of protest, and charging against political leaders, and crying out against injustice. Do these add up to thinking in mother tongue? All these border upon imperative themes.

Yes, everyone is guilty at some phase, of these themes. But then that is not all there is about the new poetry. I don't think that is all that can be found. Because highlighting these series of angry protestations locks our poetry in a box. And then when anyone looks at it, they say 'is this what it is all about?' But it is not all there is. The critic therefore must discover other new altitudes in the work of art and in discovering these, expand the frontiers of meaning. It helps us to really develop this genre, especially within the Nigerian academic system. And I think It also helps us to move further from the box in which we find ourselves enclosed at present.

GMT: Yes, you are correct in actually identifying this emerging stereotype which makes it an issue of great relevance for the poet who decides to explore his private sentiments. In fact, most of the poems we have now deal on one political issue or the other, and there is always the idea that this is because of the role of the traditional artiste in society. But I am also aware that this traditional artiste also finds time to celebrate the individual feelings. And what emerges, or what is most important, is not even that idea of celebration but how he does it.

This is where we seem to be missing the point because we are simply out to interpret. And then there is this idea that poetry serves a purpose for the community and so the poets, especially the new poets, having been identified by Aiyejina and other critics as serving a purpose for the community, all that he does must be seen from the angle of serving or achieving something for the community. If it serves the interest of the individual (because you start from self to community), this creates an unnecessary burden and critics do not bother. I think the job of the new critic is to see that there is a blend. We need to go beyond the 20th century traditional art. The 21st century traditional artiste is still here but his art has evolved; he is adapting new techniques, new devices, new ways, and new visions. The critic also has to go beyond seeing just how art merely serves community. Art also promotes aesthetics and like purpose. This is actually a very important point if we are to avoid the danger of imposed limitations ... in fact in the past our poetry had been written off as mere protest. Recently, 'protest' might even be a better term for the level our poetry might descend.

CE: Frankly speaking, the issue about what is Nigerian poetry grows tenuous when viewed from the point of quality of artistic expression. One gets bored with superfluous African images for some kind of pointillist identity. It was Osundare's pastoral poetry that inadvertently precipitated this crisis in literary creativity. The individual is taken through a whole maze of idiomatic, proverbial and intensely provincial Africanist expressions. What this does – not in Osundare's poems, but in the works of his imitators – is that it shuts out the audience, the kind of thing we find in provincial American dialogues. I don't think writers must write essentially for the African audience. So that when we have sufficiently got non Africans uninterested in our literature, we begin to shut off other ethnicities, with our provincial worldviews, with as much local idioms, local languages, and local examples as we can unearth. I think we must write for the simple reason that we feel deeply the need to give expression to that which inspires us to speak. And though we may tap quite richly from the abundant store of images that abound in African flora and fauna, but a conscious artiste, like Achebe in his novels, tries to domesticate, using a term by Nwoga, or tries to authenticate this rich repertoire of tradition within the expressive power of his message.

Of course it is a matter of choice, I am not trying to prescribe for others. All I am trying to say is that the so-called celebration of African life style, African imagery, African flora, African fauna by the younger writers who try to emulate the older ones will soon surpass itself by the inability to reach beyond our immediate province. So I will enjoin scholars to really develop a rigorous critical approach to emerging works. And in doing so they shouldn't be mere cheerleaders.

GMT: Talking about the pastoral beauty of Osundare's poetry, I think that is what Chinua Achebe did for African fiction. I see Osundare's poems, many of his poems, as very good blend of tradition. I think where the problem lies is with the poor imitators that don't really understand that, to a large extent, style is an individual thing. Because Achebe became successful in what he did in his earlier novels, it doesn't mean that we must all go imitating him in every work of prose fiction. You said Osundare precipitated a crisis, but I wouldn't call it a crisis; I would rather say that in Nigeria there are poor imitators. The very good poets and writers are those that discover themselves and forge their own styles. Many believe that since Osundare is good it follows that they must write the same way. Such imitators may flunk and bring out the worst of this style of poetry. And I think this has been the problem.

Having said that, another issue that strikes me is the idea that critics who, looking at the works of a particular poet, tend to include the whole anthology as rave success. I am very aware that all poets both within and outside Africa don't write such wonderful poems all the time. Sometimes when you review a collection of 30 or 50 poems, only about 5 make very good poems. But there is the tendency in Nigeria that once somebody brings out a collection all the poems are high success. This creates a problem. To begin with, it does not help the poet to know his weaker or finer qualities. Critics should be able to say that these poems are very good and these are not so successful. For instance, when you look at Tanure Ojaide's poems, especially the ones in *The Fate of Vultures*, I don't think that many of the poems there are as good as his earlier collections. Our critics can do better there. It should not always be the case every poem is very good.

CE: Yes. The problem here is that colonialism actually afflicted our generational psyche in the sense that we develop hypersensitivity to criticisms that bother around culture, tradition and ways of life. And if you remember Negritude developed out of that sense of outrage against the Western superiority complex. Even in traditional life, lapses are explained away as simply culture. So where you have this high level of sensitivity, you also have a lot of intolerance to honest self evaluation. 'I am black and proud' precludes any possibility of deeper self evaluation. I think that while we give credit to Chinua Achebe for having stood up to effectively decant some of the deprecatory attitudes towards Africa, that singular response has also carried a complex in the writer when he fawns excessively over what he considers to be his culture. And that is where a great disservice can been done to African literature, including its poetry. It is pathetic to hear an African say 'leave our literature alone.' Some African scholars actually put it in writing that other people should leave their literature alone, and even went further to delineate who should qualify to be the critic of African literature. You see this intolerance has done discredit to African literature. It has stultified the development of the literatures of Africa including Nigerian poetry. Now what you have are cheer leaders as I said earlier. You dare not say a writer can do better in certain instances; he takes it personally. You do not suggest ways he could have remedied his art, he says you are prescribing. You do not say a writer's work has certain defects, some will say you are jealous of his great fortune.

That is why I doff my cap (permit the expression) for Chinweizu, Jemie and Madubuike because what they did in *Decolonisation of African Literature* might not be matched now and in future. It actually took great courage to research and come up with the facts they presented us with and, till date, we are either responding to Chinweizu and company or sweeping them under the carpet with the pretence that their language was vociferous. So what do we have after Messrs Chinweizu and co? We are falling over all kinds of work. They believe that you have to lump every work as - like you said - great success. Now everything their favourite writes is the best. And many of you have barely resisted this pull too. Just like the sycophants that writers criticise in political circles who cheer political gladiators for whatever benefits, we also have intellectual cheerleaders who simply clap their hands for their favourites. There is no honest appraisal or criticism of a work and any attempt to make negative critical remarks will be interpreted as 'bolekaja.'

It is this inability for genuine introspection that has is the bane of African writing. I don't think we inherited this quality from our older writers because Achebe and Soyinka never spared themselves when it came to occasional remarks about each other's works. I remember Soyinka riling Achebe's treatment of Ezeulu's public ritual performance in *Arrow of God* as 'dogged secularisation of the profoundly mystical'. Soyinka actually had a point because in Achebe's *Arrow of God,* if one had expected a delineation of the role of Ezeulu taking mythical proportions, one would be disappointed. The role was so secularised that it lost its spiritual impact. And Soyinka was a favourite for African Spirituality. But then Achebe could argue that this was not his intention in the novel. You see this interaction of opinions, like we are doing online, develops the frontiers of literature.

But when you have people singing praises, you take up a whole volume of poetry and you think that the purpose of your work as a scholar is to shower encomiums to everything the person has written, you are doing a great disservice to scholarship. And I won't hesitate to say blurb writing is not literary criticism. So the job of developing African literature should be taken back to where it belongs. It is not the author who has deemed it fit to express within the depth of his own profundity; it is the critic whose study in great depth reveals significant findings without becoming a victim of his opinions. Our society must learn to separate their emotions or divest their personal frontiers from what is deemed public duty. This is where your new criticism should actually lend a focus.

GMT: The issue you have raised, especially when you talked about victimisation, is very important. I tend to think that many critics - particularly those in the Ivory Tower that have yet to sit on a professorial chair - cannot afford to be reckless, although this is not intended to be an apologia. My experience based on close interaction with these people shows that many tend to shy away because they are afraid of victimisation. As a result they either ignore the issue or take off on a familiar and safer tangent in their criticism. That is actually passing off something that they know is not really good stuff because they are afraid that if they speak out, they will be victimised. At least, to become a professor, one's papers have to be sent out to other colleagues in other universities. And daring to reveal the demerits of certain arguments of others who may take it out on the person isn't a very wonderful prospect.

Our problem is that we have allowed politics to creep into areas it shouldn't even be in the first place. The same political avarice creeps into the Ivory Tower when dons begin to critique from narrow, selfish ends. This is already affecting our literature. It is affecting our writing because nobody is able to tell the other the truth concerning issues and ideas because many are afraid of victimisation.

CE: Let me help you with a point on this outstanding contribution you have made. I recently had a discussion with a colleague of mine about a piece by Jeyifo on the poetry of Maman Vatsa. You remember how Jeyifo made strong points about the poor quality of writing that the late Maman Vatsa had churned out in his time as against the commendation that was paid to this poet when he was alive.

GMT: Yes.

CE: But it struck me as funny that Jeyifo waited till Vatsa was executed over his implication in a coup d'etat before he did that piece. So it is courage that we find lacking sometimes in African writing. The courage that Achebe had shown when he stood up to an intimidating Western audience and told them that he frankly didn't think that the business of African literary criticism should be cultivated in Western soil, we seem to have lost it. Achebe paid a price for his characteristic bluntness because a particular Western laurel is being denied him. But literature and art should ideally be divorced from politics and sentiments of the day. It was the same Achebe who, in one single statement, 'art for art's sake is one piece of deodorised dog shit,' very much in the manner of Wole Soyinka's intemperate 'tiger does not proclaim its tigritude,' killed the notion that it is possible to separate the business of art from social issues.

I think the time will come in Africa when we will realise that art is often distinct from political, social and economic issues. But that does not mean that the artiste has no right or should not write how he feels even if he wants to make a commentary on political issues of the day. One has good cause in Nigeria to feel so deeply about the political gerrymandering of the nation. In fact, many fictions have dwelt on the political history of Nigeria as well. At the same time, I would rather think that it is the higher business of an artiste to uplift beyond the background of what is familiar, the background in which public opinion is steeped, or the immediate issues that titillate public imagination and stimulate the journalist's reportorial appetite. At the same time the criticism of literature should develop a benign aesthetic distancing from social, political or personality issues. These issues of political and economic considerations can only become significant as the background, or the age in which a writer lived and expressed his works. The appreciation of the high and low points of art, the progression of classical qualities, must not be hinged on how relevant he has been to the society or how he is committed to society.

It is Marxist criticism which brought these confused theories and phrases like literature of social commitment. Then we had a tyrannical prescription of how literature should be. And for those of us coming out of the age of Communism there ought to be a movement towards artistic maturity in which we begin to see a trend where the literary expressions of a given period, say about a decade or two now, could make a distinct pattern of study. It is the business of the critic, the business of the scholar, to discern these patterns. It is not the business of the poet; it is not the business of the writer. The scholar discerns a certain movement, a definite pattern and whatever social issues of the day are only the background to it. So I think that the academics of Africa have been sleeping. Having successfully chased out, so to say, Eurocentric western critics, and having established an independent·form of thought, it behoves upon them to now sit back and compete with the rest of the world. When we talk about Chinese literature, Japanese literature, Arabic literature, Africa must stand in comparison and must not bring to the festival of world literatures only literatures of social protest, literature of political commitment, art of the history of Nigeria or Africa. Africans must not be so busy fighting its wars – these terribly distracting wars – that they are unable to distinguish the business of independent literary thought from that of the political organisation of the state or administration of a university.

The onus still falls back to the owners of the literature and I think that if they fail to discern a form of African writing, then two things that will emerge. You will have the crew of African writers over there in the United Kingdom or United States who will write like chips of the western block, or you will have those writers and critics completely irrelevant and acutely narrow in their outlook as if the rest of the world did not exist. So in the literary circle, academics have to sit up to know that, inverting Achebe's parlance, it is well past morning on creation day.

GMT: On the victim complex, for instance, do you remember the supposed case of Achebe and Nnolim where the latter had a paper he called "A Source for Arrow of God" and provided or claimed he had discovered sources where Achebe lifted materials for his *Arrow of God*? I know in several discussions with colleagues that they were unconvinced by the intent at mischief underlying Nnolim's approach to what would have made some investigative research. But they dared not write. Surprisingly it was only Innes, a Western scholar, who bothered about a quick rejoinder to that mischief.

CE: Well, Africa, we have to understand, is going through a lot of changes, and just like what we have at the political front being but reflections of modern states, so it seems with our writing when we talk about modern African literature, although critics will like to add up African oral literature to the equation, while others will hack back to Ancient Egypt to find African literature always there. I think that the problems that bedevil African nation states abound too in Africa's literary circle. Some of what we celebrate are actually rudiments of scholarship; at the worst we have had two extremes: chronic personality conflicts and cronyism or fawning around the hierarchy. Between them, anyway, lie some inspiring critical legacies. But both extremes do not prove any good for the development of critical standards. So, as you said, moving beyond these polarities entails a great deal of courage and, again, I will have to salute the courage of IRCALC editors for their approach to Africa's development issues. Because the imaginative approach to literary criticism will jumpstart the expansion of African writings and earn them a pride of place among the world literati.

Believe me these problems abound in other parts of the world. The United States is even a bad example to copy. There is a near total degeneration of values; the notion of arts for entertainment has been so commercialised and debased that what they parade as best selling writing, are at best, third rate thriller and a sensational culture that only appeals to the sensitivities of the American mind viz: sex, money and some profound aberrations of human nature. Even Toni Morrison plays to the gallery of the African-American stereotype in her works and this can be quite disappointing. The development of the literature of any given society can only come from few giant efforts and it takes great personal sacrifice and then a great deal of commitment for the writer to lend profound expressions not just for the sake of commercial gain or praise but for the conviction in the validity of his experience. This is what should inform literary criticism. Both the writer and critic must be convincing. You can now compare the validity of a critical presentation such as 'A Source for Arrow of God' with the purpose of such research. You can also assess the quality of any criticism with the purpose of the scholar's research. How generously has he incorporated other materials that also reflect similar or opposing expressions? How fairly has he presented his data? What other contributions to literature has he discerned from the work under review? This attitude, spearheaded by few old and courageous critical examples, will help the growth and development of African literature.

GMT: It seems the problem of literary development is not just limited to Africa. As you observed other nations have similar problems. In all things considered I don't really think that Africa or Nigeria is lagging behind so much. It is just that there are certain things which we need to correct. Some of them are the things we have discussed earlier: fear of falling in the wrong side, and not really knowing the job of the critic. I am happy with the present trend in information which has gained across national boundaries. There promises to develop a network of rich ideas with more immediate and far reaching impact on Africa than we have witnessed in the past. The coming of IRCALC and NP on the internet to offer recent perspectives on African and Nigerian literature is a good development. When we were all talking about globalisation, many have looked at it with suspicion, but the fact still remains that our could really become a small universe. Maybe part of the objective is to curb the strife and conflicts that have gone on among nations. This understanding is very important and that is where knowing and studying other national literatures becomes important too. And perhaps, through this effort, others will see how Africa interprets its literature and may join this venture with none of the condescending ignorance exhibited by some Eurocentric critics of the 60s.

CE: You are quite correct. African writing and African scholarship are all part of the evolving heritage. Yes the literature and thought of Africa could jumpstart development beyond this state of miasma, because it is the quality of thought that rules the world. Since ideas rule the world, imagination is the strongest factor that an individual can ever possess and that is why the imaginative landscape of Africa is of interest. The ability of scholars to harness ideas from which great thoughts are moulded will do great toward transforming the entire African continent.

Unfortunately we do not have to wait for political leaders, who are largely ignorant, to recognise the impact of literature in national development. We can only pray that someday a highly developed mind could climb the seat of leadership because the present crop of Nigerian and African leaders are barbarians at best. Years ago Achebe, in accepting a national honour, had asked 'what has literature to do with it?' Every student of African literature should study that essay because it highlights the role of literature in nation building. We must always be aware of the power of literature, of imagination, to shape the world and from this awareness take our job very seriously. Just like we have political leaders and charlatans who are simply there for self gratification, so do we have these elements in African scholarship. Many scholars tend see their calling as a way to earn their way through life, reel out some published works in reputable journals and have an honourable retirement. The majority of the people we have in Africa are cut from the cloak of this group of self-serving administrators and opinion leaders. But the ideas that make a lasting impact in the transformation of a continent will subsist by the satisfaction and conviction of those who propagate them. It takes an individual who is convinced and entirely satisfied with the extent of his research to cultivate his skill even at great risk to his personal comfort. And those individuals are few indeed.

In the literary terrain we mention Chinua Achebe very often because he is one among the writers who did not care about honours, recognition or personal comfort. He is one writer from Africa who holds the deepest conviction of his role and champions that cause without fear. And in doing that he has projected Africa and her literature to a respectable place in the corpus of world literatures. Icons like Achebe and Soyinka have not come very many. But a time will come when an individual or some group with similar talents and feeling will band together and start something to stampede or jumpstart our thoughts. Like *Towards the Decolonisation of African Literature*. You know it was a courageous work. It was almost too convincing and borne out of a near-fanatical sense of mission. I don't even think that modern graduates of literature in many schools today read Chinweizu et al's book. Notice how quickly some caucus among the Nigerian literati interpreted the work from tribal sentiments. But you see, the seriousness with which we do what we do will determine the extent it can carry on.

I think Nigerian poetry and African literature in general hold a more promising climate than the dwindling fortunes of Western writing.

GMT What is your advice to fellow poets, writers and critics of Nigerian and African literature?

CE: My advice is that Nigerian poetry is full of conviction even if sometimes badly expressed. If I have cause to look back at my writings, I think I will try better. Creative artistes should follow an assiduous path of literary expression. I also enjoin Nigerian poetry critics to adopt an industrious attitude in the enunciation of art, because it is the seriousness of their conviction and the bent with which they apply the task that would determine how far their contribution goes in society. And then we are not looking at immediate benefit or gains to ourselves, we are looking at furthering the universal good by which we are inspired.

So for those who have found themselves in this kind of enterprise, or for the writers who feel that their work serves for them a kind of emotional expurgation, seek within all encouragement to ensure that the zeal and courage translate to beneficial purpose. Actually that is what life is all about. As you said, the world becoming a global village means the interaction of cultures. And in this rich harvest of cultural expression, all should bring forward their best. Everyone has a great role to play in creation; the teachers have the greater responsibility to ensure that what we are bringing out to the harvest of world literatures retain the best of what we can.

GMT: Thank you very much for coming on this forum.

CE: The pleasure is mine.

New Nigerian Poetry, 2005

Notes and Works Cited
Bibliography

1-2
'Riddle me',
'Bash them'

The creative wit of Alaa's children (I-II)

NOTES

[1]Children of Alaa (more popularly Umualaa) are part of a larger autonomous community in Umuahia South local government of Nigeria's Abia State. They are believed to be offspring of one father called Alaa. Alaa himself was one of the many sons who migrated with wives and children some miles away from Itu to the present location. Migration motive remained uncertain but may have been the usual land dispute or need for expansion.

[2] Oldest living member of Alaa community in 1986 when the interview was given.

[3] Local bard from a line of master-performers.

[4]There could someday be a computer program for riddle games with visual animations to provide a whole new breath of fresh air from the western junk that dominate the African market. But that would come when the people of Africa have learnt to take cultural dynamics more seriously than the penchant to simply assimilate whatever the western world throws at them with little or no regard for their genuine needs and sensitivity.

[5]Answers to some riddles: *Kon ti/ kon kon ti.*= Oso mgbada/ bu n'ugwu (The hare races best on a hill); *Ereghe re -ti rere* = Onye etila aki n'ogwe (Crack not kernels/ near a pit); *kpom ti/ Kpo.*= Anaghi agba/ Ose na-anya (We do not rub /Pepper in the eyes); *kpom ti Kpo* = Ikwe n'odu (Mortar and Pestle); *Kpum/ Yoooo* = Aka nkwu (Noise of falling palm fronds); What made a noise ('kpam') and ran into

bush? = Ugba (Oil-bean seed); The lamp which travels around the world = Moon; The queer woman/ who keeps her children/ in the heaven (or) the foolish maid / that breast-feeds children / over the rafters = Paw-paw tree); What fire / the snake / would never fear = Twilight; The carpenter / of long boxes = De Mike; 'Piakam-Piaaa!' = A satire of two lovers, meaning 'Theresa and John are on bed.'

WORKS CITED

Abdulkadir, Dandatti. 'Oral Composition: A historical appraisal.' *Oral Poetry of Nigeria*. Ed. J. Abalogu. Nigeria Magazine: Lagos,1980.

Azonye, Chukwuma. 'The Formulaic Character of the Oral Epic Songs of the Ohafia-Igbo.' A paper presented at the second International seminar in Igbo Literature, University of Nigeria, Nsukka, August, 1981.

de Graft, J. C. 'Roots in African Drama and Theatre.' *African Literature Today* 8. 1970.

De John. 'Performance of Riddle-Bash.' An Interview. Alaa: August, 1986.

Don John. 'Riddle Contests in my Time.' An Interview. Alaa: August, 1986.

Egudu, Romanus. 'Oral Poetry.' *Introduction to African Literature*. Ed. Ulli Beier. London: Longman, 1979.

Finnegan, Ruth. *Oral Literature in Africa*. London: Oxford University Press, 1970.

Hagler, Iyorwuere. 'Performance in Oral Poetry.' *Oral Poetry of Nigeria*. Ed. J. Abalogu. Nigeria Magazine: Lagos,1981.

Hymes, Dell. 'The Concept of Performance.' *Oral Poetry*. Calabar: March, 1986.

3-4
'Igbo Mind',
Music, Culture and Tradition (I-II)

NOTES

[1]See Thomas Hodgkin. *Nationalism in Colonial Africa.* London: Frederick Muller, 1956. p.25.

[2]The words of Igbo literary scholar Emmanuel Obiechina as cited by T. Uzodinma Nwala. *Igbo Philosophy.* Lagos: Lantern Books, 1985. p.16.

[3]Nwala, Uzodinma T. *Igbo Philosophy.* p.16.

[4]K. Onwuka Dike.*Trade and Politics of the Niger Delta. An Introduction to the Economic and Political History of Nigeria.* Oxford: Clarendon Press, 1956.

[5]Michael Crowder. *The Story of Nigeria.* London: Faber and Faber, 1962. p.28. Crowder also argues: "there appear to have been a general similarity between the Nigerian Stone Age and that of East Africa." p.27.

[6]In this catacysm waters parted, rivers turned to deserts while landmasses separated, throwing new mountains from the crust and separating surviving peoples from their homelands. See Immanuel Velikovsky. *Worlds in Collision.* New York: Pocket Books, 1977.

[7]See Cheikh Anta Diop: *The Cultural Unity of Black Africa:* London: Karnak House, 1979.

[8]For further reading of radical Afrocentric works from varied religious, philosophical and literary disciplines, the following are very useful supplements: Mbiti, John. *African Religions and Philosophy.* New York: Praeger Publishers (1969); Diop, Cheikh Anta.*The Cultural Unity of Black Africa.* London: Karnak House (1979); Soyinka, Wole. *Myth, Literature and the African World.* London: Cambridge University Press (1976); Awoonor, Kofi. *The Breast of the Earth,* New York: Nok Publishers (1975); Chinweizu. *The*

West and the Rest of Us. London: Random House (1987); Enekwe, Ossie. *Igbo Masks: The Oneness of Ritual and Theatre* Lagos: Nigeria Magazine (1987); Emezue, GMT. *Comparative Studies in African Dirge Poetry*. Enugu: Handel Books (2001) and Asouzu, Innocent. I. *The Method and Principles of Complementary Reflection in and Beyond African Philosophy*. Calabar: University of Calabar Press (2004).

[9]Taken from an interview of Fela by Tchal-Gadjieff now part of a Video CD captioned *Fela The Legend*. This undocumented VCD was on sale throughout Nigeria soon after the death of the Afro-jazz king.

[10]The Nigerian present still comes to mind with Fela Kuti's "Yellow Fever" musical track which raves at the black woman that deigns to bleach the skin, perm the hair and wear a wig in imitation of Asian, European and American cultures.

[11]Ikenga R. A. Osigbo. *A History of Igboland in the 20th Century*, Enugu: Snaap Press, 1999. p.130.

[12]Due to the tradition of European and American civilisers of the world whose Christian ritual of confession and forgiveness, both before and after the wrong, is seen to take care of every premeditated evil against another, the Nigerian politician could afford to cart away millions of public wealth after swearing to the contrary by the Bible or Koran, while his traditional religious counterpart can expect serious reprisals from his more fearsome judicious deity.

[13]Ford Johnson's *Confessions of a God seeker* (Silver Spring: One Publishing Inc. 2003) and Barbara Thiering's *Jesus the Man: A New Interpretation from the Dead Sea Scrolls* (London: Corgi Books, 1992), among similar works, are valid discussions and experiences on fraudulent religious histories in Christianity and some New Age religious traditions of the world.

[14]More recently, Ita O. Bassey's "Pharaoh a Devil?" (*Nigerian Chronicle*: April 15-21, 2009. p.20.) expounds some of the arguments of Tibetan scholars and religious Lamas, notably Tuesday L. Rampa, regarding misrepresentation of ancient historical events by some

Jewish pesharists and scribes of the first century A.D). These fringe scholars note how Egyptian technology had actually offered the beleaguered neighbours economic respite from starvation and its astrological science provided the basis of many ancient knowledge and predictions regarding events and perturbations in the then known world. But the scribblers of holy scripture hid these facts and also the existence of one of the oldest and still extant of the Seven Wonders of the World in bible records.

[15]Nwala, Uzodinma T. *Igbo Philosophy*. p.13

[16]All comments are taken from interviews from the Video Disc, *Morocco Vision 2000*. Awka: Sammy Sparkle All Stars Ltd., 2000. All translations are the writer's.

[17] Barbara Thiering's radical interpretation of the Dead Sea Scrolls reveals eloquently that the Qumran community records were forbears of the tradition of early Christian communities in AD 12 -40.

[18]This is common with Igbo traders and public luminaries whose smarting of English phrases are usually sprung into the language most times consciously and sometimes not.

5
And Tortoise flew

WORK CITED

Emezue, G.M.T., "Children in the Wilderness: A discourse on Children's Literature with Professor Anezi Okoro." Ed. Charles Smith. *African Literary Journal*. B4, 2003 (41-59).

Okoro, Anezi. *Flying Tortoise*. Enugu: Delta Publications, 2004.

6
A story of courage

WORK CITED

Pauline K. Davids. *Opuliche*. AI: Handel Books, 2008

7
Teacher's art

WORK CITED

Joy. M. Etiowo. *Mma and other poems.* Lagos: Handel Books, 2006.

8
Close strangers

WORK CITED

Judith Lutge Coullie (ed). *The Closest of Strangers: South African Women's Writing.* Johannesburg: Witts University Press, 2004.

9
Some ending narratives

WORK CITED

Bettina Weiss (ed). The End of Unheard Narratives: *Contemporary Perspectives on Southern African Literature.* Heidelberg: Kalliope Paperbacks, 2004.

Index

D